The Canadian Small Business Owner's Guide to Financial Independence

The Canadian Small Business Owner's Guide to Financial Independence

A comprehensive retirement and succession planning guide for professionals and small business owners

Barry and Mark McNulty

INSOMNIAC PRESS

Library and Archives Canada Cataloguing in Publication

McNulty, Barry, 1974-
    The Canadian small business owner's guide to financial independence : a comprehensive retirement and succession planning guide for professionals and small business owners / Barry McNulty.

Includes index.
ISBN 1-897178-20-4

        1. Retirement income--Canada--Planning.   2. Businesspeople--Canada--
Finance, Personal. I. Title.

HG179.M3667 2006   332.024'014'0971   C2005-907631-3

The publisher gratefully acknowledges the support of the Canada Council, the Ontario Arts Council and the Department of Canadian Heritage through the Book Publishing Industry Development Program.

Printed and bound in Canada

Insomniac Press, 192 Spadina Avenue, Suite 403
Toronto, Ontario, Canada, M5T 2C2
www.insomniacpress.com

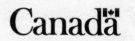

We would like to take this opportunity to thank the team of people we work with for their support and understanding while we prepared this book.
Their contribution was invaluable!

We would also like to acknowledge the input of Ms. Susan Megson for her assistance in converting our experience and philosophical approach into this book.

Table of Contents

Introduction

When I was young, I used to think money was important.
Now that I am older, I know that it is.
–Oscar Wilde

In the course of your lifetime, you'll go through many types of transitions. They're a fact of life. Some happen naturally, such as the progression from childhood to adolescence to adulthood; others require decision making and appropriate follow through. When it comes to your business and your financial independence, taking the time and actions necessary to plan for your transition is vitally important. It's not something to leave to chance!

Imagine that you're taking a long drive to a remote location you've never been to before. Would you load the family into the car one beautiful morning and start out without any preparation? Not likely. Nor would you want to leave without being sure of such important facts as the condition of your car or your ability to get sufficient fuel and food along the way. When it comes to embarking on this type of journey, you know that being properly prepared makes good sense. If you're familiar with driving a car on a long journey, it's easy to understand the importance of preparation and planning.

Planning the journey from business owner to contented retiree, however, isn't something you do regularly. Throughout your lifetime you'll likely do a transition of this type only once. That's what makes appropriate preparation all the more important. After all, dealing with your transition to retirement is a lot more complex than planning a car trip.

From Independent Business Person to Independent Retiree

Popular wisdom and most of the books available address the aspects of life that affect most Canadians. Consequently, there aren't many comprehensive road maps to guide you in dealing with the additional complexities entailed in going from independent business owner to independent retiree. It's a lot different than retiring from a job with a pension. As a business owner, you definitely have unique needs (and hopefully opportunities) compared to the majority of Canadians.

You have a business to run and hopefully, although this is not always the case, a business to sell at some point, with all the complexities that entails. Financially speaking, entrepreneurs and professionals generally have more flexibility in managing their income and Cash Flow than someone with a regular job. Typically, you also have a need for more sophisticated tax planning, particularly at transition time. Unlike employees, who have available to them such programs as deferred profit-sharing plans, stock option plans, and pension plans, those who are self-employed must bear the responsibility themselves for building a relative level of financial independence.

Questions You Might Have About Your Transition

- How do I go about planning for my transition?
- What are the potential problems or pitfalls I should watch for?
- Will I be able to count on selling my business interests? If so, for how much?
- Have all appropriate tax strategies been considered for my circumstances?

- Have I fully defined my retirement vision?
- What is the cost of a retirement lifestyle that I will feel satisfied with, after tax and inflation?
- Do I have enough capital today to be financially independent or do I need to build more wealth?
- Just how much money will I need, anyway?

Helping you find answers to these questions and others is why we wrote this book. We want to provide you with a road map to help you be proactive and plan the transition that's right for you. While you're on this journey, you won't be alone. A 2005 CIBC World Markets study entitled "Are Canadian Entrepreneurs Ready for Retirement?" shows that about five hundred thousand small business owners and professionals are planning to retire over the next five to ten years. Transition planning will be critical for all of them. The good news, if you're in this group, is that there should be an increasing number of services available to help you meet your needs. The bad news is that you can't wait for these services to evolve. If your transition will take place within the next five to ten years, our view, based on twenty-five years of experience working with business owners, is that you need to start developing your transition plan now. Depending on your circumstances, it can often take many years to effectively "get all your ducks in a row." The CIBC study reveals that only about 40% of business people have a well thought out plan on how they're going to manage their transition. Worse still, of the group who do have a plan, many have only dealt with the issues that affect their business. This is not a complete transition plan. A properly constructed plan has three phases, as outlined below.

1. The Pre-Transition Phase: This is the stage when you build the relative level of financial independence you're going to need to retire and live in a lifestyle in

which you'll be comfortable. Think of it as the organization and preparation phase when you determine how you're going to exit effectively from your business. Depending on your circumstances, this phase can take up to ten years or more.

2. The Transition Phase: This is the stage when you find a buyer for your business, assuming you're in the type of industry or profession where this is possible, and deal with all the resulting legal and tax issues. This is when you'll have to decide if the monetary offer for your business is appropriate relative to the assumptions used in your overall transition strategies. If you're not going to sell your business, but rather just "close up shop," it's during this stage that you'll have to deal with your staff, the disposal of fixed assets, outstanding debt, accounts receivable, and so on.

3. The Post-Transition Phase: Unfortunately, many business owners don't plan adequately for this phase. It's important to consider that if you're in relatively good health when you retire, you might wind up living for as long as or even longer than you worked. It's absolutely essential to the success of your transition that this phase therefore be properly incorporated into your strategies. The consequences of not including it can be disastrous for your life planning and lifestyle. If you fail to build the appropriate level of financial independence during the pre-transition and transition phases, the resources you'll need to maintain a satisfactory lifestyle for the rest of your life might not be there. Running out of money in your late seventies or eighties is not a pleasant situation to contemplate.

Finances Play a Key Role in Your Transition

Everyone's transition preferences are individual, but for most people, financial considerations are the key to their decision making. After all, money is more than just a medium of exchange in our society. Human beings tend to be concerned with "status," and money (or the lack of it) has a strong influence on one's place in society. It's a fact of life that if you're financially successful, your friends, colleagues, neighbours, and even family are more likely to admire and respect you.

Financial success even has a strong influence on how you view yourself. Without sufficient money, you might not have the freedom to live your life to the fullest. Financial stress can be difficult to bear, especially in your later years when you no longer have the earning ability to create new wealth. It can affect your health, your relationships, and even your ability to provide security for yourself and your family from life's random challenges. Of course, it's important to keep in mind that money is relative. What's sufficient for you might not be enough for another person.

Your Transition Team

While it might be tempting to organize your transition on your own and thereby save some money, this is not the best decision in our experience. You can't do everything yourself. You have a business to run, and for most people, that's a full-time activity. Furthermore, you'll need to access the specialized expertise offered by professionals in order to optimize your alternatives. Our advice is to create a "transition team" made up of a variety of professionals, each of whom will provide services during the three phases of your transition. A typical transition team would include an accountant, insurance representative, lawyer, investment advisor, banker, business valuator, business broker, and other professionals as needed.

To function properly, every team needs a coach to coordinate its activities and to help it focus on the same goals and objectives. This person organizes everyone's special abilities and talents into a cohesive group. Our book will help you fulfill the important role of coach as it relates to your team. This will allow you to create the appropriate level of financial independence you need for your ideal transition. You can choose to act as coach yourself or you might wish to delegate this responsibility to one of your trusted advisors. But keep in mind that delegating doesn't mean abdicating!

Regardless of the approach you take, this book will facilitate your understanding of the transition process. You'll know what questions to ask, what concerns should be addressed, and how to recognize existing opportunities that will give you greater control over the process. In short, this book is intended to put you in the coach's box so that you can personally control your own transition.

Types of Transitions

It's important to remember that transitions come in many forms with multiple variations. Some people plan on selling their business and retiring to their idea of the good life, without ever looking back. Others prefer the idea of a staged transition where they sell part of their enterprise, allowing them to slow down while at the same time continuing to enjoy the benefits of ownership. Still others choose to sell out, but do so with the proviso that they can continue to work at the company for a specified period of time. Six months or one year are common when the purpose is to facilitate the transfer of goodwill to the buyer, but other arrangements may involve a much longer period of time. We can't cover all the variations and permutations in one book, but the basic steps and information should be of assistance no matter what your transition preferences.

Case Study

"Bill" had established his business in a small community about an hour's drive from a major urban centre. He was in his early fifties, married, and had four children, ranging from seven to sixteen years of age. He had an established, profitable proprietorship and was in good shape financially. While he didn't want to stop working entirely, he did feel the need to slow down a little and take some time to "smell the roses." His problem, however, was one of growth. The community had expanded quite a bit over the past few years. The result was that he was busier than ever. Bill had tried bringing on a couple of extra staff but that hadn't proved to be the answer. His facilities, located in a small house he had purchased twenty years ago, were getting cramped and they were out of room. Renovating or moving would be an expensive undertaking. At this stage of his life, Bill was rightly concerned that he might not be able to recoup on his investment for an expansion or renovation by the time he wanted to retire.

One alternative was to simply reduce his hours and stop taking new customers. This would, however, create a negative impact on the value of the firm he'd worked so hard to build over the years. It would also open the door to unwanted competition. He was proud of his accomplishments at the office, and letting the goodwill value deteriorate didn't feel right to him. Thankfully, Bill's story has a happy ending. He decided to sell the business for a good price to an ambitious, young entrepreneur, who was more than happy to keep Bill on as an employee. The result was a seamless win-win arrangement.

The Six Step Transition Planning Process

Step One: Establish your destination (or your goal for financial independence).

In detail, formulate and define what you want from

your transition and what your vision is for your post-transition lifestyle. The chapter on goals will help with this part of the process.

Step Two: Determine your starting point.

Where are you today, financially, in both a business and personal sense? Referring back to the analogy of taking your car on a journey, it's important to know your exact location before you even get into the car. If you don't know where you are now financially, how can you effectively plan a journey to your desired destination? Rest assured, this book includes some helpful guidance on figuring out your starting point.

Step Three: Identify your transition strategies and list them in order of priority.

This is where you decide, given your resources, how you can get to your chosen destination. This could include business building strategies, tax strategies, investment strategies, income management, and more. Incidentally, you've probably heard the expression, "Life is what happens while you're making other plans." We use this expression frequently in the book because it helps to bring home an important concept: the need for contingency planning strategies. Contingency planning may involve an emergency succession plan with your employees, insurance, liquidity reserves, partnership or shareholders' agreements, and more.

Step Four: Break your long-term transition plan into twelve-month Action Plans.

Doing this allows you to incorporate your long-range goals into current business plans and personal financial management.

Step Five: Monitor your progress.

This is critical. We advise you to monitor your progress on at least a quarterly basis so that adjustments to the various aspects of your transition strategies can be made in a timely manner.

Step Six: Perform a yearly review and establish a new twelve-month Action Plan that incorporates the previous five steps.

Over twenty-five years of experience and refinement have gone into the transition planning strategies explained in this book. Throughout the years, the business owners with whom we've worked have found these strategies to be a successful template, and we trust you will too.

Managing a busy enterprise along with enjoying a rewarding personal life takes good time-management skills. Out of respect for those skills, we've written this book using a streamlined format to ensure that the information is easy to understand and apply to your own personal situation. If you're acting as coach to your transition team, you'll find that it provides a handy game plan.

Finally, we're all individuals, and a good transition plan should be customized to suit your particular needs. One size fits all is not the best approach when it comes to your transition. In this book, we discuss a system for planning your transition that has proven successful over the years. Some of the strategies mentioned in these pages will be right for your circumstances and some of them won't be. Therefore, it's very important that you check with your team of professional advisors when considering any of the strategies discussed within these pages.

Now let's begin....

Chapter One
Goal Setting

This chapter will help you:
- **Understand the importance of well-defined goals in transition planning,**
- **Appreciate the value of prioritizing your goals,**
- **Quantify your goals in current dollar terms,**
- **See the impact of time as a variable in your goal setting.**

Your transition is a major milestone in your life. In a sense, you're the architect charged with the responsibility for the design and shape of your future, so it's important that you plan for a transition that's right for you as a unique individual.

In the introduction to this book, we outlined the Six Step Transition Planning Process that we've used successfully with our clients over the years. The first step in the process requires you to formulate your transition goals, or, put another way, define what you want from your transition. This step should also include a definition of your post-transition needs, so that you end up with a complete picture of where you're headed.

McNulty's Coaching Advice
Define what you want in a way that gives meaning to your ongoing strategies. Consider it a way to translate your dreams into your goals. Then think of

your goals as the foundation upon which you build your strategies. Ultimately, it's by implementing your strategies that you get what you want. You shouldn't have goals without strategies. Strategies are the bridges that take you from where you are today to where you want to be.

Ten Key Steps in Formulating Your Transition Goals

Below, we've summarized ten key steps in formulating your goals in a manner that will enhance the transition planning process.

Step One: Define Your Goals in Specific Terms

Successful goal setting is all about giving definition, shape, and structure to your individual dreams. When it comes to defining the transition you feel is right for you, there are many possibilities, variations, and combinations to choose from. Let's look at the pros and cons of some of the more common types of transitions.

I. Full transition – outside purchaser

In this instance, you fundamentally sell your business outright. This doesn't mean that you necessarily stop working the day after the sale closes. Whether you're selling shares of your company, a professional practice, or your dry-cleaning store, you may continue working. You would, however, be an employee or perhaps an associate. What we find today is that many business owners or independent professionals don't want to stop working once the business is sold. Working, particularly on a part-time basis, often helps people "ease" into retirement life. Keep in mind that the purchaser might also want you to stay on to help facilitate the transfer of all that goodwill you've built up with existing clients or customers.

The pros:

- You get all your money out at one time.
- There are no continued staff or management responsibilities. (Being able to go home at a normal time and close the door on "the daily hassles" because they're now someone else's problem can be very appealing.)
- You pass on responsibility for care of your enterprise quickly and efficiently.

The cons:

- The change might be too rapid, with no time to "ease into retirement."
- You lose any entitlement to future growth and profits; the return on capital for a well-run business or professional practice generally can't be duplicated with passive investments at an acceptable level of risk.
- If you're in a small community or have a specialty practice dependent on referrals or are in a competitive business environment, you need to keep your plans confidential until you have a firm purchase agreement in place.

II. Full transition of a closely held corporation or a partnership to other shareholders or partners

In this case, you get the best results by obtaining an independent third-party valuation. You might also want to hire a facilitator as part of your transition team to rough out the basic terms of the transition. You'll also be in a better position to instruct your lawyers and accountants on what you want.

The pros:

- You get all your money right away.
- Typically, you have more control on the timing of your exit.
- You're relieved of staff and management responsibilities.

- There's often a higher level of confidence that the business you and your partner(s) have built up will continue.

The cons:
- If you've been in business or practiced with someone for a long time, personal feelings and expectations can cloud important negotiation issues.
- Some agreements that have been in place for a while might have buy/sell provisions that aren't appropriate in today's market. We once worked with a client who had been in a partnership for over thirty years. When the agreement was put in place, goodwill had little real value and it stipulated that the buyout price would be based on the value of the tangible assets only. You can avoid such disputes by keeping your practice agreements up to date.

Did You Know

The demographic realities of Canada in general, and the small business sector in particular, suggest that succession planning is increasingly becoming a critical issue. According to CIBC World Markets, by the end of the decade, an estimated $1.2 trillion in business assets are poised to change hands—the largest turnover of economic control in generations.

III. Partial transition of a closely held incorporated business to an employee or employees and/or active minority shareholders

The best way to deal with the issue of price, especially if the purchaser is a member of your family, is to obtain an independent opinion from a qualified valuator. Valuation firms often advertise in business or professional journals, or you could get a referral from a professional or business association or from an advisor such as your accountant. When you're considering a professional succession of this nature, it's important that all parties have the feeling that the final terms result in a win/win arrangement. If one or more parties consider in retrospect that they didn't get a fair deal, resentment can develop and seriously affect your future success. For this reason, you might also want to retain the services of a professional facilitator.

The pros:
- You're able to slow down and possibly take more holidays.
- When selling shares, you ideally have committed members of your team with whom to divide up the workload.
- You can delegate with more confidence.
- You spread around your financial risks.
- Selling off some shares can improve liquidity and free up capital for other uses.
- With the right shareholder agreements in place, you can provide for death and disability buyouts and even include wording that will facilitate your final succession to retirement.
- You continue to benefit from your proportional share of profits.
- There can be greater potential synergy.

The cons:
- You have to consider the other shareholders' opinions when making decisions.
- If you have delegated an area of responsibility, you'll have to be prepared to live with their decisions even if they're not the ones you would have made.
- With other shareholders, tax planning becomes more complicated.
- Once someone is a shareholder, it can be difficult to deal with disagreements, and arrangements are harder to unwind than set up.

- Your entitlement to future profits and growth of the business or professional practice is reduced or diluted.

Case Study

Over the course of thirty years, "Steve" had built up a trucking firm in southern Ontario. With a lot of hard work, he and his wife "Lorraine" (who was not a shareholder) had taken the business to a point where they employed close to sixty people. For most of this time, Lorraine had handled the administrative side of the business. When she reached a point in her life when she no longer wanted to put in the long hours and hard work, Steve still wasn't willing to pack it in, though he did wish to slow down a little. Frankly, the thought of running everything himself, without Lorraine, was a little unsettling to him. At the same time, there were two employees who had been taking on increasing responsibility. Both were making a significant contribution and Steve and Lorraine felt very comfortable with them.

After a lengthy discussion, a deal was reached with these two key employees that would see them become shareholders. Steve had his recent year-end financial statements on hand which showed the "shareholders' equity." The agreement was that each of the two employees would buy 24% of the outstanding shares of the company by paying 24% of the shareholders' equity; all four shook hands on the deal and the employees had their lawyer draw up a letter of intent to this effect.

Unfortunately, things began to fall apart when Steve told his accountant about the deal. The accountant explained that due to goodwill and a number of other factors, the business was worth significantly more than the shareholders' equity figure shown on the balance sheet. The result was that after a lot of stress for the whole company, the two employees resigned and went to a competitor. It was a very unhappy experience for all parties.

IV. Partial transition of an independent professional practice to an associate – cost sharing

In this type of transition, an associate buys client files or patient charts and a share of the office's tangible assets (equipment, leaseholds, etc.). Generally, he or she is then entitled to all the revenue from production as it relates to these clients or patients. Expenses are typically shared through a pre-set formula, such as having each party pay an equal portion of fixed costs and a proportional share of variable costs based on production.

The pros:
- You might be able to slow down without negatively affecting the value of your practice.
- Some of your capital in the practice is freed up either for investment or some other purpose that serves your longer-term strategies.
- There is better coverage when you're on holidays.
- Management duties can be shared.
- You have the benefits of synergy.
- On a cost-sharing basis, you have greater independence as compared to a partnership.
- Buy/sell arrangements can be put in place to protect the value of your practice from contingencies.
- You still get to enjoy the benefits and profits that come from practice ownership.
- There's a logical potential buyer for your remaining practice when you're ready to do a full succession.

The cons:
- You must consider another party when making decisions.
- There could be conflicts in practice philosophy or other disagreements that aren't apparent before the associate has "bought in."
- You lose the benefit of profiting from the associate and the hygiene production on the patient base that's purchased by him or her.

V. Partial transition of an independent professional practice to an associate – partnership

Under a cost-sharing arrangement, you have separate practices. A partnership is different in that only one practice exists. Basically, the members of a partnership work together and share everything including patient ownership and profits. There can be many formulas for the sharing of profits; they can be split on a 50% basis or even shared proportionately relative to production. Some partnerships work on a formula whereby each partner keeps all of his or her personal revenue (less expenses) and the only sharing that's done is on the profits generated by associates and other staff members.

The pros:

- You spread out your financial risks because your partner or partners are there to share the investment and costs.
- There's better coverage when you're on holidays.
- Management duties can be shared.
- You have the benefits of synergy.
- Buy/sell arrangements can be put in place to protect the value of your partnership interest.
- You still get to enjoy the benefits and profits that come from practice ownership.
- There's a logical potential buyer for your remaining practice when you're ready to do a full succession.

The cons:

- As partners typically share everything, you have less flexibility for independent action. For example, you might be required to work a minimum number of days in the office or produce a minimum level of production.
- Resentment and potential conflicts can develop if one partner is not living up to the expectations of the other partners.
- Disagreements can be more stressful because of the close relationship of the involved parties.

VI. Partial transition – selling a portion of the business

This concept only works when the business can be segmented into different portions that can be clearly separated from the whole.

Case Study

A retailer named "David" had built up a business that included a number of locations. The managers of these individual locations had an understanding with David that when he wanted to slow down or retire, they would have the option to purchase their own store.

In another case, a sales agency had a number of successful product lines. When "Betty" wanted to slow down, two product lines were sold off, with the cooperation of the manufactures they represented, to the top salespeople on that particular item.

This concept works for certain independent professional practices as well. In dentistry, an associate could be brought into the practice with the express understanding that he or she would buy their patient charts (representing goodwill) when they reached a minimum level (800 to 1,000 charts, for example) and then move out of the office.

VII. Merging your corporation or partnership with a competitor or someone in a similar business

Mergers can be a very complex and challenging way to implement a transition. The pros and cons are a combination of those listed above under sections I. and II. Issues to address revolve around valuation of both of the businesses, management and operational control, retention of employees, potential pre-merger liability, and contingent liability. If you're considering such a transition alternative, be sure you have a strong transition team with a lot of experience in such transactions.

VIII. Merging your independent professional practice with a younger member of your profession

This concept works well if you have started to slow down and have reached a point where it's no longer practical because of your declining patient or client load to justify your own office and staff. Moving in with a younger practitioner who has some extra room often means that you can continue viably in practice. These arrangements are typically set up so that your overhead is all, or mostly, on a variable basis. Rather than paying a fixed cost, you pay the younger practitioner a percentage of production. In turn, he or she provides the facility, staff, and so on. We recommend that you negotiate a purchase arrangement for your goodwill prior to moving in. Once you move in, it could be difficult to move out if you and the younger professional can't agree on terms.

IX. The "fold your tent and walk away" transition

Many entrepreneurs and independent professionals find themselves in this position. Unfortunately, they didn't address value management issues and transition planning early enough. They don't want to move in with or merge with another practice or business, and they find that their operation has little in the way of commercially transferable goodwill. At the same time, business might have dwindled to the point that it doesn't justify operating on their own. If you find yourself in this position, the hope is that you've set aside enough money so that you have a relative level of financial security. On one hand, you won't have to deal with the complications of selling your practice or business. On the other hand, it's a shame to have worked all those years and receive nothing for it when you decide to close the doors.

In deciding what you want in a transition, ask yourself the following questions:

- What would be the ideal age for you to do a full transition?
- Would you consider a partial transition?
- If you would consider a partial transition, would you prefer a partnership, a cost-sharing arrangement, just selling goodwill or a portion of the business, or perhaps some variation thereof?
- What are you going to do with your free time once you "retire"?
- Where would you live?
- Would you consider giving up your Canadian residence?
- Do you want to develop another career entirely? Full or part time?
- How much after-tax Cash Flow will you need to finance your ideal retirement lifestyle?

Let's take a closer look at that last question: How much after-tax Cash Flow will you need to finance your ideal retirement lifestyle? You might find it difficult to estimate what your retirement lifestyle costs are likely to be. As a guideline, consider what your lifestyle costs are today (a simple system called "Banking by Objectives" can be found later in this book to help you with this process). Once you know what your lifestyle costs are today, you simply reduce this figure by expenditures that should be eliminated by that time such as education and support for the kids, debt service, some insurance costs, and RRSPs or individual pension-plan contributions. You might also have to add some costs such as those associated with an expensive hobby, travel plans, etc. Don't forget to include an estimate for contingencies, such as car replacement.

In short, what you're trying to identify is your retirement lifestyle needs in today's dollars. This information is then combined with estimates on: time to succession, longevity, inflation, investment returns, taxation, details on your investable assets that relate to ownership, and the ratio of RRSP or pension plan assets to non-registered investments. This will make it possible for you and your transition team to quantify how much retirement capital you're going to need.

A qualified retirement planner should be one of the people you enlist for your team early in the pre-transition stage. They can perform the complex calculations you will require. To fulfill this important role, the planner must understand what strategy alternatives are available. They should also know how to estimate your needs; have knowledge about annuities, reverse mortgages or variations thereof, and registered retirement income funds; how best to manage Cash Flow in retirement; when to encroach on capital; and so on.

Make sure the retirement planner is also comfortable dealing with estate-planning considerations. We recommend someone with a minimum of a CFP designation (Certified Financial Planner) who has experience working with clients who are independent professionals and/or small business owners. We also recommend that this member of your team work on a fee-for-service basis as opposed to being compensated by commission earned from the products they sell. We're not saying that people who make their living on a commission basis aren't capable or ethical, it's simply that there are important decisions to be made based on the expertise of this valuable member of your transition team. You want to be certain that the recommendations are motivated by what's in your best interests.

In the next chapter, we'll discuss what we call your Current Position. Having quantified the amount of money you're going to need to finance your retirement, you'll be able to see whether your current resources are sufficient or if you'll need to build additional wealth. Here, again, a qualified retirement planner should provide valuable input. They should be able to tell you whether your resources are sufficient to provide for your future needs. If you need to save more or create more wealth, they should be able to tell you exactly how much and ideally how to go about it. We'll look at this topic again in later chapters.

Step Two: Ensure Your Transition Goals Are Realistically Attainable

Setting attainable goals is quite motivating. They can invigorate you and provide more purpose to your day. Such goals can even enhance the satisfaction you feel from working, when you see yourself achieving these objectives. Setting goals that are *not* realistically attainable can, and usually does, have the opposite effect. They're nothing more than a recipe for frustration.

Why would a goal be unrealistic? From a financial perspective, it has to do with what can be thought of as a "Resource Gap." In other words, you don't have the money, assets, or earning ability to get where you want to go. That's why the next chapter, "Establishing Your Current Position," is so important. It will help you develop a solid understanding of what your financial resources are today. After all, *you need good information to make good decisions.* Knowing where you are today is a prerequisite for developing workable transition strategies.

Step Three: Prioritize Your Goals

Unless you expect to inherit great wealth, you probably have finite financial resources. That means you have to focus those resources on what you have identified as your most important goals. Sounds easy enough, doesn't it? The difficulty arises when you have to select which goals are "most important." We recommend that you set no more than three to five prioritized goals. Having too many goals can dilute your focus.

Step Four: Break Down Goals into Their Appropriate Component Parts

You have no doubt heard the old saw, "How do you eat an elephant? One bite at a time." Most large goals can be broken down into components that make them easy to relate to and achieve. To be useful in setting transition strategies, financial objectives need to be broken down in a meaningful way. Let's assume your planning indicates that you'll need to increase your gross income by $30,000 per year. Expressed in this manner, this might seem like a daunting objective, but if you're an independent professional working on a fee-for-service basis and you work 240 days per year, this is only an extra $125 per day.

Let's take the example of a manufacturer. Assume your cost of goods together with the marketing, general, and administration expenses typically run you about 90%. To increase your personal gross income by $30,000, you would need to sell an additional $300,000. That's an additional $1,250 per day using the assumption of 240 working days per year. That might be a big increase, perhaps even impossible. One thing is for sure, however: breaking down this number to what you would have to do on a daily basis will make it far easier to come up with strategies to achieve this objective.

Here's another example. Assume that you have to save $25,000 per year over and above RRSPs to build the wealth you'll need for your transition. It must also be assumed that you have the Discretionary Cash to meet this objective, otherwise we'd be back to working out strategies to increase revenue as described in the previous example. Either that, or you'll have to change your transition goals to a level that is realistically attainable in your business or profession. By Discretionary Cash, we mean after-tax funds that aren't committed. After all, you can't decide to stop paying for normal day-to-day living needs, debts, and so on. Discretionary funds are those monies about which you can make choices. Once again, a large goal like this is difficult to take action on. Breaking down this figure to a more manageable level, such as savings of $500 per week or $2,083 per month, is the secret to turning your financial goals into reality.

Step Five: Integrate Your Business or Practice and Personal Goals

If you're like most of us, your business or professional practice is going to be the engine that drives your financial train. This is where you earn your personal income. We consider the following a Golden Rule of financial management for owners of closely held businesses or professional practices: *either your business/practice must support your personal needs or your personal needs must be adapted to what the business/practice can support.*

When owners of closely held businesses or professional practices run into financial trouble, it's often because they didn't integrate their revenue-earning activity and personal planning. If you decide to spend money on office renovations, it'll affect the Cash Flow you have available for personal use. If you decide to renovate your home, the money generally must come from your business or practice.

McNulty's Coaching Advice

Your personal financial life and your business are intimately linked. Therefore, it's prudent not to commit to strategies in one part of your life without making sure that these strategies complement the other.

Step Six: Put Your Goals in Writing

Unfortunately, memory is short and easily distorted. To illustrate this point, let us recall an experiment we did in grade school. The teacher whispered a statement into the ear of one of the children and had each child whisper it into the ear of the classmate next to them until everyone in the room had heard it. The interesting thing about this experiment is that the statement whispered into the ear of the last child was nothing like the one the teacher first passed on. It became distorted in the telling.

Putting your goals in writing is the best way to avoid this kind of distortion and to formalize the process. It also cements the commitment. If in the course of time you forget how your goals are prioritized or a specific detail about any of them, you can simply refer to what you've written down. Committing your goals to paper also facilitates the measurement of your progress (or lack thereof) over a period of time.

In addition to stating your goals in writing, we recommend that you include the strategies you wish to use and the time frames you intend to maintain. If other people will be responsible for carrying out a part of any strategy, make a note of that too.

Step Seven: Communicate Your Goals to Other Interested Parties

Business takes teamwork. If your goals involve the business, the specifics should be communicated to your team through your business plan. But this doesn't mean you have to tell them personal details or share private information. For example, if you and your advisors determine that you need to produce an additional $300 per day to reach your objective, you would simply share this objective with them. This will help them take on some of the responsibility and buy into the goal. It will also help you define your expectations of them: you'll know when they're doing a great job and when they're not.

Naturally, it's a good idea to fully involve the home team in your goals too. It will strengthen commitment and ideally enlist the whole family in reaching the objectives.

Did You Know

A quick look at the numbers suggests that self-employed people rely on RRSPs more than regular employees. In fact, almost 70% of small business owners own RRSPs compared to 55% of paid employees. Those who are self-employed also contribute more to their RRSPs, with the average annual contribution being just over $6,000.

Step Eight: Review and Regularly Revise Goals

Consider setting aside what we call "B" time, at least biannually, to review your progress and strategies. "B" time is when you handle important activities that aren't urgent. If your strategies involve increasing gross business revenue, we suggest reviewing it more frequently, perhaps quarterly.

Monitoring your progress is critically important! The best time to find out that you're *not* meeting your goals is when corrective action can still be taken. Waiting until the end of the year to find out that you didn't make your income targets leaves you without any options. However, if you find out in the first quarter of that year that you're not on target, it's still possible to make some adjustments to achieve your objective.

In addition to monitoring your progress, use a "B" day late in the year for an in-depth review. Doing so will allow you to incorporate what happened during the past year with the outlook for the coming year so that you can establish new meaningful goals for the coming twelve-month period. You might even find that your goals have changed. Or maybe you have decided that you would like to try a staged transition where an employee or associate is brought in on the basis that they'll be buying part of the business. If you weren't able to find a suitable candidate or if you entered into such an arrangement that didn't work out, then you might want to change your transition goal to a full transition model.

In addition, you might decide that you need more money for your retirement living needs. Also, tax rules and the economic outlook might change. By reviewing your goals and strategies regularly, you'll be able to adapt them in a timely manner so that you can reach your ultimate objective.

Step Nine: Make Contingency Plans

In planning for the future, the expression, "Life is what happens while you're making other plans" should be taken to heart. No one knows what challenges the future will bring. That's why it's important to have emergency funds available for things such as home and auto repairs and the necessary replacement of office equipment.

For larger contingencies, make sure you have appropriate amounts of life insurance, disability insurance, office overhead insurance, and personal property and liability coverage. Critical illness is another form of coverage you might want to consider. It's also advisable to make contingency plans to protect the goodwill in your business.

Step Ten: Consider the Non-Financial Implications of Your Transition

Transition from your business to retirement will require more than just an orderly disposition of the business and the financial wherewithal to support a comfortable lifestyle. When you think about it, there will be upwards of two thousand hours of time to fill per year. Unless you plan how to fill this time in a manner that you'll find rewarding and satisfying, your retirement could be a disappointment. Studies have shown that retirement can have deep emotional implications that can affect your health, marriage, and other relationships, even your lifespan.

Those who are most successful with this aspect of their life's transition are those who approach it like they approached their business. Being happy and contented in retirement takes effort! We can't tell you how many clients have confided to us a year or two after retirement about how much they miss their business or practice. They had great visions of playing golf, relaxing down south in the winter, and spending time at the cottage in the summer, but the reality is that you can only play so many golf games per year (or at least that's true for some of us). Also, relaxing down south can get pretty boring after a period of time unless you have some satisfying activity to use up all that energy that used to go into your business. Therefore, you might want to add someone who works as a "life planner" to your transition team.

We hope we've impressed upon you how important it is to formalize your goals and strategies. It's the first step on the road to your future happiness, and if you get off on the right foot, you'll find the journey easier and more enjoyable.

Chapter Two
Establishing Your Starting Point – Cash Flow

This chapter will help you:
- **Understand the importance of Cash Flow,**
- **Know how much money is available from your business to finance your personal needs,**
- **Know how to figure out your personal living expenses (PLE),**
- **Work with your transition advisory team to establish this key transition planning information.**

The Starting Line

Where are you today in a financial sense, relative to your transition and retirement goals? The hope is that you've built up assets such as a valuable business, RRSPs, and other savings. But will it be enough? Or will you need to set aside more money, and if so, how much? To answer these important questions, you must first understand what your financial resources are likely to be over the next twelve months. We call this establishing your Current Position. Think of this initial process as the starting line for your transition planning.

Let us draw an analogy between the importance of determining your Current Position and the navigation of a ship. If you were the captain of a vessel on the west coast of North America with the intention of sailing to New

Zealand, there's a piece of information that you must have before you can accurately plot your course. It's the precise location of where you are going to start your journey. In an example like this one, the importance of knowing from where you're starting your journey is pretty obvious, and the same is also true for a meaningful transition plan. It's important that you understand your present financial health for planning this journey as well. Your Current Position is your starting point for any transition strategy.

Establishing your Current Position requires that you understand two general categories of information. The first is your Cash Flow: what money comes in and what money goes out. The second is your Net Worth: what you have and what you owe in terms of assets and liabilities. We'll cover Net Worth in the next chapter, so first let's turn to Cash Flow.

The Importance of Cash Flow

Cash Flow is one of the greatest financial resources owners of mature businesses have (we're assuming that you didn't win the lottery or won't inherit great wealth in the near future). For example, if your business is currently grossing $600,000 per year after cost of goods sold, but before general and administrative expenses and profit, and you have ten years to a full transition, assuming inflation will average 3%, you can expect to have a total inflow during this period of $6,878,327. That's a lot of money going through your hands. Decisions you make on how these funds will be spent could affect the outlook of your business, the financial security of you and your family, and the success of your long-term transition plans.

Cash Flow is an important resource but it's typically not well understood. This is unfortunate because if you can't understand it, you can't manage it! Thankfully, understanding the business component of this valuable resource is fairly straightforward. There are many established systems that can tell you what happens to your income and expenses at the office (year-end financial statements, tax returns, and so on). But from then on, it's typically a black hole as far as reliable information is concerned. Don't worry, though, as you'll see, there's a simple way to develop the attention to detail that you'll need to understand what happens to your cash. The place to start is with your business.

Let's begin by putting your mind at ease. You don't have to be a mathematician, accountant, or MBA to establish your Current Position or figure out your Cash Flow or Net Worth. You'll probably just need to know how to direct the appropriate members of your advisory team and make sure they have the right information to make the right decisions. On the other hand, if you're preparing your own Current Position, you'll find the following information useful in guiding you through the process.

Fundamentally, to develop the Cash Flow component of your Current Position, you would use historical information, which we'll discuss in a moment, combined with your expectations of what's going to happen over the next twelve months.

Step One: What Money Comes in and What Money Goes Out – The Business

At this stage, we want to know how much pre-tax money is available from the business to finance your personal needs. To begin, you must identify your gross inflow of funds. In a service business or professional practice, this can be fairly straightforward. It's your gross collections in a given period (not to be confused with gross fees or sales). For a manufacturer, retail operation, or other enterprise that involves the sale of a product, it can be a little more complex. What you are looking for is gross collections less cost of goods sold. This figure will tell you what funds are available prior to general and administrative expenses, income taxes, non-cash expenses, and, of course, profits. These collections represent your inflow of funds. General and administrative expenses and income taxes (excluding non-cash expenses) make up your business' cash outflow. Non-cash expenses, by the way, include amortization or depreciation. This is an allowance provided for in the Income Tax Act that recognizes that the value of your tangible assets, such as equipment, declines over time or with use. Think of it as a deduction that reduces taxable income without you *directly* having to pay out any money.

Proprietorships and Partnerships

For an unincorporated business where there are no affiliated corporations in place, the process is relatively simple. We suggest for reference that you use your most recent year-end Profit and Loss Statement, also known as an *Income and Expense Statement*. This document is historical in nature, so where appropriate, make any adjustments for the present year. To do this, ask yourself the following questions:

• Will gross production be the same, higher, or lower?
• What will change from an expense perspective? If you anticipate a change in gross production, don't forget to make a corresponding adjustment to variable expenses (shipping costs, supplies, and so on).
• Will any leases mature?
• Did you retire any material amounts of debt which would reduce interest costs?
• Did you hire any more staff?
• Have any other costs gone up or down?
• Do you plan to buy any equipment or incur any capital expenditures over the next twelve months?

Adding your accounts receivable for the last fiscal period to your estimated collections this year or period, less expenses and current accounts receivable, should give you a pretty good estimate of what your business Cash Flow is. If you're in a partnership, we would recommend that you multiply this figure by your percentage of ownership to arrive at an estimate of available Cash Flow.

Incorporated Businesses

Corporations, as they relate to Current Position, are in some ways only another entity for tax purposes. This is important to understand. Money earned in the corporation doesn't automatically fall into your personal income for tax or Cash Flow purposes, as does the net from a proprietorship or your share of partnership profits. Earnings in a corporation may not necessarily be paid out in the present year. Some business owners accumulate earnings not needed for their personal lifestyle in their companies. It's a good place to save surplus funds not needed for working capital purposes for your goals. (We'll look at this concept in more detail in the chapter on tax strategies). Nonetheless, for our purposes here, it's still a financial resource that's at your disposal. Think of it as having your funds in different pockets, with the corporation simply being another pocket.

Step Two: Personal Cash Inflow – What Comes In

Summarize all net income sources, including:
• net business income or salary,
• income your spouse earned,
• non-cash expenses, if available, from your unincorporated enterprise or partnership,
• dividends,
• anticipated interest income, proceeds of any borrowings personally or in an unincorporated business activity, and
• any other inflow of funds, such as gifts, proceeds from the sale of property, and so on.

Step Three: Cash Outflow – What Goes Out

Income Tax – Definitely in the Outflow Category

Ask your financial advisor or accountant to calculate the tax for you. He or she will need details about your income expectations for the coming period. Computer programs are so sophisticated today that given the right information, your financial advisor/accountant should be able to work out a figure suitable for planning purposes in minutes.

Personal Lifestyle Expenditures (PLE)

Don't be concerned if you don't immediately know what your personal lifestyle expenditures are or how to go about calculating them. You're not alone. Most people would be hard pressed to provide anything other than a rough estimate (that's often not even close) if asked to come up with this figure. A simple Cash Flow management and monitoring system we've used effectively with many clients is called Banking by Objectives (BBO). It's described below. By the way, if you're making quarterly tax payments, you might want to set up a tax account within your BBO system so that you can deposit funds on a monthly basis

Perhaps you share our view that the most important money you have is what's left over after all expenses. This is the money that finances your lifestyle, educates your children, and builds your future financial security. Understanding your PLE is therefore critical. A saying we believe to be very appropriate here is, "If you can't understand it, you can't manage it!"

PLE includes all expenditures for your lifestyle. A little further on in this chapter, we'll look at some simple systems for identifying these numbers. Please be aware that we're not asking you to prepare a budget. In today's society, the word *budget* has negative connotations, the same way the word *diet* does. Very few people enjoy the idea of a constraining personal budget, so you'll be happy to hear that the answer to controlling your finances and reaching your objectives is not cutting back on your personal lifestyle. If it turns out that you don't have the Cash Flow or other resources necessary to meet your goals and expectations, the most successful solutions have proven to be increasing net revenue in the business or changing, perhaps marginally, your goals or time frames.

But first we have to understand what it costs to finance your lifestyle in order to evaluate whether or not your revenue is adequate for all your needs. Having this information helps you take control of your financial future. Such control can only come with strategies that are appropriate for your individual circumstances.

PLE represents funds that you've committed to paying out. They're similar to fixed expenses in your office, and they don't include discretionary expenditures or savings. PLE examples include food, shelter, and transportation costs, along with expenditures for your children's needs, loan payments, and insurance premiums for *necessary* coverage.

McNulty's Coaching Advice

PLE should also include clothing, entertainment, vacations, and even pocket money for you and your spouse. With respect to pocket money, ideally your PLE should provide sufficient money so that you and your spouse can meet your personal spending needs without being accountable to each other for how the money is spent.

How to Determine and Manage Your PLE

There are many ways to determine your PLE and some are more involved than others. Over the years, we've experimented with them all. One important point: this is not something you can effectively delegate to your transition advisory team.

If you like working with a computer and you have the time to do the data entry, software programs can do the job extremely well. It can, however, be challenging to come home from a busy day at the office and spend an hour or two entering details of your personal and household accounts into a computer.

Another way to determine your PLE is through the Banking by Objectives (BBO) system. BBO allows you to identify your money with its intended use, which is part of the reason it's successful as a Cash Flow monitoring system. In fact, it's the system my (Barry's) mother used when I was a young child. I remember that she always had wrinkled beige envelopes in her purse. They went everywhere she did. Eventually I discovered how effectively she used them. There were things she wanted or needed for either herself or the family and to manage the saving process, she created this system of envelopes. She had separate envelopes for house repairs, vacations, clothes, and so on. She identified the money contained in those envelopes with its purpose and whenever she wanted to know how she was doing on that priority, she simply pulled out the envelope and counted the contents. Certainly, there are more sophisticated systems for managing your cash. On the other hand, hers worked—and worked simply. She would consistently reach her goal.

BBO is based on this system. It's a simple feedback system that can also be enlarged to encompass other priorities, such as taxes. To use BBO to establish your PLE, follow these two steps:

1. Go through your cheque books and credit-card bills for the past twelve months. Remove any non-recurring discretionary items. Are there any personal expenses that you've paid through the office by credit card? At the end of the year, your accountant would typically allocate these expenditures to your personal draw, so these funds are definitely part of your PLE; they should be factored in as well. To this amount, add any anticipated increases in expenditures.

For example, has your mortgage payment gone up? Did you lease a new car? Perhaps your house taxes decreased—okay, that's unlikely!

Now you're ready to divide this total figure by twelve for a general idea of your average monthly PLE. This is the figure you would initially use in estimating the Cash Flow portion of your Current Position. It's an important number, so we would recommend you use the BBO system to confirm the estimate as outlined below.

2. Confirm your PLE estimate using the BBO system. Just set up or designate an existing bank account as your PLE account and arrange for it to be covered by overdraft protection. Now let's say your review of cheque books and credit-card statements indicated that you spend $7,000 per month on PLE. For the next year, deposit this amount into the PLE account each month (using any time schedule that's convenient). All identified PLE outflows should then be paid for from this account. Don't take the money for any PLE item from any other account. Even credit cards used for items that would be categorized as PLE expenses should be paid from here.

Now You Have a Simple Feedback System!

If your PLE account is always going into overdraft, you'll know by how much your initial estimate was out. Or conversely, if a surplus builds up, you'll know how to adjust your PLE estimate.

By establishing a realistic PLE, it should also be possible to determine how much money, if any, you have left over. To arrive at this important number, deduct your PLE and the income-tax estimate from your total anticipated inflow for the year. We refer to what's left over as your Discretionary Cash, and it's generally very small in relation to the amount of money that has flowed through your hands (including your company) from all sources. Yet it's still important because this is the only money you can really make decisions on. After all, you can't decide to stop paying staff salaries or suppliers at the office, nor can you stop paying for food, clothes, or shelter. For the most part, you're committed to many expenses before you even earn the money.

Determining your level of Discretionary Cash (or the lack of it) is critical to sound transition planning. Your resources are finite. When you don't identify your level of Discretionary Cash, it's easy to spend it on secondary priorities, often on impulse. By identifying the cost of your goals, Discretionary Cash can be allocated from the outset towards achieving them. This means you're taking care of your essential priorities first. From this point on, you can spend the rest of your income knowing that you've already taken care of your most important commitments.

Chapter Three
Establishing Your Starting Point – Net Worth

This chapter will help you:
- **Understand the uses of a Net Worth Statement and how it's prepared,**
- **Know the importance of classifying your assets and liabilities by type and ownership,**
- **Appreciate the connection between your Cash Flow and Net Worth,**
- **Be aware of valuation terms and methods as they relate to your business, and**
- **Know how often your Net Worth Statement should be updated.**

In the last chapter, we discussed your Current Position as a starting point for your transition planning. Your starting point can be thought of as a two-sided coin. On one side of the Current Position coin, you have Cash Flow, which we dealt with in the last chapter. On the other side of the coin, you have Net Worth, which includes what you have and what you owe.

Think of Net Worth and Cash Flow as being linked together in a dynamic sense. Any Cash Flow you generate after tax that isn't spent on perishables (items without lasting value) will impact your Net Worth. For example, money spent on vacations or dining out can provide great personal value, but, unfortunately, it won't add to your asset base as represented by your Net Worth. On the other hand, Cash Flow used to purchase a house, car, investments, or to build a savings account will affect your Net Worth. These are tangible assets. When you use your Cash Flow to acquire tangible items, you're simply changing the character of a resource from a very liquid tradeable commodity to another form of asset. Long-lasting financial security and wealth is best built when part of your hard-earned Cash Flow has an impact on your Net Worth.

Your Net Worth Statement

You have no doubt heard the expression "a picture is worth a thousand words," and in our experience, that's definitely the case when trying to understand a client's assets and liabilities. We find it useful to think of a client's Net Worth as just that: a picture or a snapshot of what they have and what they owe *at a particular point in time*. The preparation of a Net Worth Statement could reveal some interesting financial information and it's also a critical part of establishing your Current Position or starting point for planning purposes.

Your Net Worth Statement provides a picture of what you have to show for all your hard work over the years. It's called a Net Worth Statement because deducting your liabilities (what you owe) from your assets (what you have) tells you how much you're worth in dollar terms, on a net basis. Your Net Worth picture can provide vital information for your transition. Let's take a quick look at three specific ways it can help you.

1. It can help you understand the present makeup of your Net Worth

When you do a full transition, at some future point you'll be dependent on the Cash Flow that your assets will generate to finance your lifestyle needs. It's important to look at the distribution of the assets that make up your Net Worth. In short, you need to establish what are potential revenue-producing assets and what are not. Let's look at an example of why this is important:

Entrepreneur A has a Net Worth of $1,500,000 with 30% of the assets of a personal-use nature (and unlikely to generate Cash Flow after transition).

Entrepreneur B has a Net Worth of $2,000,000 with 60% of the assets categorized as personal or non-producing.

Question: Which entrepreneur has greater financial security, assuming lifestyle needs are similar?

Answer: Entrepreneur A. What counts is not only the size of your Net Worth but also how well it's organized relative to your needs and goals.

McNulty's Coaching Advice

If a large portion of your Net Worth is invested in a house and you're planning, as part of your transition, to sell it and move into a less expensive place, we'd advise caution. In all our years of working with business people, we've seen very few cases where this strategy has proved to work satisfactorily. While conceptually the idea seems good, if you're used to a certain quality of living, it's very difficult, in practice, for you and your family members to reconcile to something less. Certainly, there's no problem selling your larger home and moving to something smaller. However, you might find that the funds generated from the sale are largely used up on features that will make your new home feel more comfortable.

2. It can facilitate long-term tax planning

Income splitting and tax deferral options are cornerstones of tax planning in Canada. How investable assets are split between spouses, the relative weighting of registered assets (RRSPs/pensions), non-registered assets, corporate assets, etc. can all have an impact on how much tax you pay. It's ideal to have a mix of assets that have different tax consequences when you are eventually living off the income and/or capital. We'll cover this topic in more detail in a later chapter. For now, whether you're preparing your own Net Worth or having it prepared through your advisory team, make sure your assets are categorized by type and ownership (what's in each spouse's name or joint title). Doing so will be useful to you and your advisors in planning strategies for both your transition and eventual retirement.

3. It can provide a tool to measure your financial progress

Let's assume that a year ago you prepared your first Current Position as part of a long-range transition plan. Your goals, based on Cash Flow expectations at that time, were to save $2,000 per month beyond RRSP contributions for your financial security, $300 per month for your child's education via an RESP, and to reduce your debt by about 20%. It's now twelve months later. The only way to know whether or not you should be congratulating yourself for accomplishing your objectives is to compare your present Net Worth Statement to the one you prepared a year ago. It's also the only way you can properly gauge the impact of returns or losses on your existing investment assets in relation to your overall financial security.

As another example, suppose when you first prepared your Net Worth, it was apparent that the available investment assets of one spouse were substantially greater than the other. This is not a desirable position for long-term tax-planning purposes. Your savings strategy at the time would likely have been to build up that additional wealth in the name of the spouse with the lower investment base (see chapter eight for tax strategies). Did the strategy work or didn't it? The only way you can really be sure is by updating your Net Worth. Think of it as establishing a new Current Position for the following year's strategies.

How Often Should a Net Worth Statement Be Prepared?

A new Net Worth Statement should be prepared every twelve months—at a minimum. Why so often? It's not just because you need to monitor your progress. The other practical reason for this frequency is that you and one or more members of your advisory team will have to prepare a new twelve-month plan for the coming year. In effect, you're creating a new starting line. The secret to accomplishing a long-term objective is to break down the actions that must be taken into "edible bites." Similarly, a long-term transition plan is best accomplished with a series of twelve-month action plans that move you toward your objective.

When you and the appropriate advisory team members do your comparison with the Net Worth Statement prepared last year, you might find that your Net Worth grew more or less than expected. Perhaps some investment returns were better or worse than expected or you had expenses that lowered your savings, or maybe you earned more than you anticipated and your savings were greater than planned. It's unlikely you would find everything worked out exactly as expected. Transition planning is dealing with the future, which none of us can see with any real clarity. You have to constantly make adjustments to allow for the unexpected. Preparing this picture of your assets and liabilities at least every twelve months will help you know what adjustments need to be made for the following year's plan.

A Net Worth Statement is therefore a vital part of establishing your Current Position or starting line because it provides you with information that's integral to the success of your transition strategies. We can't stress enough the importance of completing and using this financial tool effectively.

Preparing Your Net Worth Statement

Here are some steps to guide you through the process:

Step One: Pick a Date

Remember that your Net Worth is a snapshot of what you have and what you owe *at a particular point in time.* The date you choose (in consultation with your advisors) should be the same day each year. We recommend you select a date where information will be readily available, as opposed to some arbitrary timeline. An example would be December 31st, or if you have a non-calendar fiscal year-end for your business, that date would also be suitable.

Step Two: Organize Your Information

You'll have to assemble your "stuff" on your chosen date. By "stuff," we mean:

- all bank statements (corporate or business and personal),
- investment statements,
- confirmation of outstanding balances on debt (both corporate and personal),
- value estimates for your business,
- value estimates for real estate,
- actual cash surrender value (after all redemption charges and penalties) of whole life or universal life contracts, and
- values on other assets such as limited partnerships, other active business interests, art, stamp or coin collections, and so on.

In some cases, accurate values may not be immediately available. While it's important to get this information right, keep in mind that you're not preparing audited financial statements. If the information is not available, it doesn't mean you can't proceed. In some cases, you have to make estimates. Do the best you can with the information available. When making estimates, do so on the conservative side. This is an area where it might be a good idea to get some additional input from your advisory team.

When it comes to other personal-use assets such as furnishings, cars, or boats, simply make an estimate of their value. They have little or no impact on transition planning because they don't appreciate in value and will never generate any income.

Step Three: Complete Your Net Worth Form or Have It Completed for You

Once you've accumulated the data or "stuff" you'll need, you can begin completing the Net Worth form. A sample can be found in the appendix to this chapter. If you're having it prepared by a member of your advisory team, make sure they understand how you want the information organized. It would also be wise to agree on a deadline for its completion. A new Cash Flow projection should be prepared at the same time.

Defining Some Categories

Most of the asset categories on your Net Worth Statement are self-explanatory, but some require additional comments for clarity.

Cash. This category does not include registered (RRSP/ Pension) or corporate cash. Cash in your RRSP or corporation normally can't be withdrawn without tax consequences. Technically, cash would be allocated to reserves for emergencies or expenditures that are anticipated within the next twelve months. This is also a good place to track uncommitted cash that has accumulated. This category doesn't include cash reserves that form part of your long-term investment portfolio, as these funds are committed to a longer-term purpose. It would therefore be recorded as part of your registered or non-registered investment assets. All you are trying to identify are the cash reserves that are available for liquidity purposes.

The Business. If you have had a valuation prepared recently by a qualified valuator, then you would enter this figure. A professional valuation is the most accurate way to determine what your business is worth on the market. Some professional valuators offer an update service that you might find advantageous, particularly if you're within five years of succession. The update is annual and the cost is nominal compared to a new valuation.

If you haven't had a professional valuation prepared (our recommended course of action), there is a method we use for deciding on what figure to use on a client's Net Worth Statement for the business. Let us stress that this is not an opinion of value in the traditional sense. Many factors go into determining the fair market value (FMV) of a commercial enterprise for sale purposes. Rather, this is a way of trying to identify what the business is worth to you, the owner, as an investment. FMV can also be useful as an ongoing measure of value management in planning transition strategies.

The calculation involves "capitalizing" the net earnings of the business. In brief, you take the net normalized profits (explained later) that the business generates and divide it by a factor that compensates you for both the risk level you undertake in ownership and for the lack of liquidity. To illustrate this point, consider an investment that's generating a profit of $40,000 per year. If you wanted to earn 12% on your money, how much would you pay for the right to receive this $40,000 per year? The answer is simple. Divide $40,000 by 12% ($40,000/.12). The price you would pay in order to get 12% on your capital would be $333,333. To confirm the accuracy of this calculation, multiply $333,333 by 12%. If you felt there was a greater risk of receiving this $40,000 per year, you might demand a greater return in order to induce you to invest.

Doing the Math
We recommend that the appropriate member of your advisory team perform the calculation to determine the value of the business to be used on the Net Worth Statement, particularly if you are incorporated, as the tax impact of a sale of shares versus an asset sale must be considered. To understand the process, the value estimate for purposes of your Net Worth would generally be calculated as follows:

Step One: First normalize operating results (on a consolidated basis if you have more than one corporate entity) by taking the profits from your financial statement and adding back the following:

• Tax planning, such as salary to a spouse or children over what you would have paid an arm's length person for the same work;
• Lease payments or financing costs because whether or not you have invested cash or financing, you are liable for what is invested in your business. What we're trying to determine is the real return on that capital;
• Allowances for personal expenses, such as your car, personal travel, unusually high continuing education costs, etc.

Step Two: From the adjusted profit calculated in step one, deduct an amount for your personal contribution to revenue and management. You basically have two things that are at work in your business: you and your capital. Keep in mind that the value we are trying to determine relates to the return on your capital, *not* on your personal production. To make an accurate assessment of real profit, there has to be some recognition of the fact that part of your time, as an owner, must be devoted to management in addition to production. This can be difficult to measure. You could take your hourly production rate and keep track of how many hours you have to spend weekly and/or monthly on management-related activities. You would then multiply that figure by your hourly production rate to assess a logical management allowance. But this requires a lot of time and effort. Instead, you might want to simply factor in what it would cost to hire a fully arm's-length professional manager.

Cash Surrender Value (CSV) of Life Insurance. This is another entry that might require some explanation. Have your insurance agent provide you with a letter advising what the actual CSV is as of the date you've chosen to prepare your Net Worth Statement. It's important to define CSV as the amount you would receive if you asked for a cheque. Insurance contracts and terms can be complex. We've seen many policies that state that the owner's CSV is subject to redemption charges and/or surrender charges (normally in the small print) and these charges can be significant. This is particularly true of policies that have been in force under five years. We recently had a client ask what his CSV was on his policy. He was told that it was $29,000. He then asked whether this was the amount of the cheque he would receive. It wasn't. The actual amount of the cheque would be $1,500. This is a big difference that can impact your savings plans and investment strategies.

Some Rules of Thumb for Net Worth

Rules of thumb are general guidelines, so please consider these comments accordingly:

Rule 1: If you have any non-deductible debt, make paying it off a priority. There are no investments of which we're aware that can provide as good a return, after tax and with as little risk, as paying off non-deductible debt. For example, if you have a non-deductible loan at 7%, assuming a top marginal tax rate of about 46% (in Ontario), you would have to get a pre-tax rate of return of about 15% to equal it. Where can you get an investment with that kind of return and no risk in today's world? To pay off $5,000 of non-deductible debt, you have to earn, on a pre-tax basis, about $10,700. Ideally, part of your transition plan should be the elimination of all debt, but particularly non-deductible debt, prior to your transition.

Rule 2: If your debt level, whether deductible or not, is 40% or greater than your asset base, we strongly recommend that you concentrate your resources on reducing it.

McNulty's Coaching Advice

If you have extensive debt relative to your assets, run, don't walk, to a qualified financial planner or accountant. You'll want to talk to someone who does more than simple tax returns and financial statements but who won't try to sell you various financial products.

Rule 3: Build levels of liquidity (cash reserves) to the point where they will cover at least six months of living expenses plus any major purchases anticipated during the six-month period. This provides the security to meet most contingencies not covered by insurance. Many entrepreneurs we know feel they don't need to worry about reserves because they have available lines of credit. Maintaining enough cash to handle anticipated purchases is a good way to manage your spending. Don't accumulate non-deductible debt that will hinder your transition planning.

Rule 4: If you have tax arrears, consider borrowing the money to bring you current. Even if the borrowing will be non-deductible, the costs will be lower than what the Canada Revenue Agency charges.

Rule 5: If you have credit-card debt that can't be paid off monthly, borrow from the bank to repay your high-interest balance.

Rule 6: Where possible, if you have non-deductible debt as well as deductible debt, have all principal repayment directed to the non-deductible debt and arrange for the deductible liability to be on an interest-only basis until there are no longer any non-deductible obligations.

Rule 7: Many of the books written on financial advice today recommend that you build the RRSP levels for each spouse so they are equal in value. This advice is reasonable as a general rule for the majority of the population. For most successful business people, however, it would be preferable to make sure that the total amount of investable assets, including an allocation for the proceeds of your eventual business sale, are balanced between spouses. In many cases, there can be a great disparity between the income of the business owner and his or her spouse. Without forethought, the result can be that investable assets build up disproportionately in the name of the business owner. That is not ideal from a transition planning perspective (see chapter eight for tax strategies).

Once you've had your Net Worth Statement properly prepared, you will be well on your way to determining your Current Position. On a practical level you'll have an excellent understanding of how your assets and liabilities are organized. In addition, you'll have a useful tool for establishing strategies, addressing problem areas and tax planning, and measuring your progress. Ideally, establishing your Net Worth should leave you feeling empowered and ready for the next step in planning your transition.

Chapter Four
Introduction to Financial Independence and Transition Strategies

This chapter will help you:
- **Understand the difference between Wealth Creation and Wealth Management, and**
- **Learn how to determine which strategies are best suited to your unique circumstances.**

When approaching transition strategies, it might help to build a mental image of them as bridges that take you from where you are today to where you want to be in the future. That's why in the preceding chapters, emphasis is placed on goal setting and establishing where, in a financial sense, you are today. Getting your bearings places you in a powerful position; it equips you to create effective strategies and bridges to a future that is right for you.

Wealth Creation and Wealth Management

It's important to differentiate between Wealth Creation on the one hand and Wealth Management on the other. Most of us think of the word *wealth* as a term that applies to the very rich. That's not the case in this context. The definition used here relates to an individual's or family's assets of a non-personal nature. This excludes the house, for example, the car or home furnishings and other assets of that nature. Let's look at some definitions to make things clearer.

Wealth Creation involves actions that create or harness the Cash Flow and other resources you need so that they can be organized strategically to meet your defined goals.

Wealth Management involves strategies which are intended to ensure that what you have is optimized and protected, to the greatest extent possible, from losses that can occur through undertaking greater risk than necessary, inflation, taxation, or lack of focus. Depending on your individual Current Position, your strategies might emphasize Wealth Management alone or Wealth Management in combination with Wealth Creation. All of the strategies discussed in this chapter fall into one or the other of these two categories.

Wealth Creation and Wealth Management strategies are most effective when they're properly coordinated to complement each other. When you own your own business, Wealth Creation strategies are centred on that enterprise. Wealth Management strategies, on the other hand, are intended to complement the wealth you create. The whole purpose of Wealth Management is to optimize what you have and to maintain the integrity of the capital or relative wealth that you've built up. It makes no sense to have effective Wealth Creation strategies if the money is lost.

What Best Applies in Your Situation: Wealth Creation or Wealth Management?

After defining and quantifying your goals (see Step One in chapter one) and determining your Current Position, you'll be in one of the following three positions:

1. You *do* have sufficient capital today to meet your identified needs and goals given reasonable assumptions. This definition includes either having the funds today or the asset base which, if left to grow, would reason-

ably be expected to reach the required level. Of course, this is the best of all possible scenarios. If this describes your situation, you should be emphasizing Wealth Management. Wealth Management strategies are a combination of income management, tax planning, investment strategy, and risk management (insurance, estate planning, business agreements, business contingency plans). Each of these strategies should be coordinated so that they complement one another and are focused on your prioritized objectives. It's also important that you monitor your position to make sure nothing happens to change this outlook.

2. If your current capital were invested, it would *not* likely grow to the point that your assessments have identified as being necessary. However, you and/or your advisors have calculated that you *do* have the discretionary levels of cash needed to meet identified savings. Keep in mind that Discretionary Cash simply means that you have after-tax income that's not spoken for in advance. In other words, you don't require this money for things such as lifestyle needs, debt repayment, educating your children, and so on. Without some form of disciplined savings plan in place, discretionary funds tend to be spent on secondary priorities or impulse purchases. Overall, if you're in this situation, employ a combination of Wealth Creation and Wealth Management strategies.

3. You *don't* have either the asset base or the Discretionary Cash today to meet your identified objective. Many business owners find themselves in this position. If you find that you fall into this category, don't be disheartened. There are alternatives. When you first assess your Current Position relative to your long-term objectives, it can be a real eye-opener. Should you find yourself in this position, your choices are:

a) Create the additional wealth you need. This would be done through a combination of improving the business' bottom line, emphasizing proactive tax planning (see chapter eight for tax strategies), income management, and savings strategies. You may have noticed that we didn't include "improving investment returns" as one of your alternatives. Generally, in the investment world, to realize greater returns you must undertake greater risks. In the long run this can be counterproductive. For a more in-depth discussion on this topic, see chapter nine on investment strategies.

b) Reduce your personal spending. In our view, this is the least effective alternative. When you've been accustomed to a certain lifestyle, it's hard to be satisfied with less. Over the years, we've found using strategies to increase income are much more effective. The exception relates to tax planning and/or debt reorganization. Poorly organized debt is often a major reason why entrepreneurial families don't have the Cash Flow available for their long-term Wealth Creation needs. Thankfully, even little changes in the way your debts are structured can work wonders on your Cash Flow. We'll look at this issue again in a later chapter.

c) Change your transition objectives. The more money you want to live on after transition, the greater the sum you'll have to accumulate. The closer you are to your transition objective, the more aggressive your Wealth Creation strategies will have to be to build up identified shortfalls in required retirement capital. Alternatively, you can always decide to change the parameters of your goals. You could decide to live on less in retirement and/or do your transition later than originally planned. Both of these changes have the potential to bring your objectives into line with your resources, or of bridging what we refer to as the Resource Gap.

Other Transition Considerations

What follows is a number of transition considerations you might want to address, depending on your circumstances.

Investments in Equipment

If you're seven to ten years from transition, should you be making any investment in improvements to the business? For example, new equipment or leaseholds will often increase the marketability of your business. If you think something needs to be changed prior to your transition, talk to the business valuator on your team. Many business people wait to spruce up their office, modernize their facilities, or replace old equipment until just prior to their full transition. In effect, they're "getting the business ready for sale." While this can help facilitate a faster sale, it's not always a good financial decision. Depending on the useful life of the asset or improvement involved, you might want to consider investing earlier rather than later.

Staff

Talk to the legal member of your advisory team well in advance of your transition date. You want to be sure you understand how to handle your duties and obligations as an employer and plan accordingly.

Make Sure Your Agreements Are in Good Shape.

Do you own shares of a corporation which has other shareholders? Is there a cost-sharing arrangement in place? Are you in a partnership? A common problem we see with these types of agreements that can affect transition planning is the wording of the first right of refusal. The majority of these agreements we review require the party who wishes to sell to first offer the other party or parties to the arrangement his or her shares or interest in the partnership or business.

If the other parties to the agreement refuse to buy, the wording in these agreements doesn't leave you free to easily seek another buyer. Why? Because any change in the final price or terms typically requires the vendor to go back to their shareholders, cost-sharing associates, or partner(s) and again offer them the right to buy. Generally, this must be done in writing and you typically must provide them with a period of time, thirty days, for example, to make up their mind and get back to you. In principle, this doesn't sound too bad, but practically speaking, it can present a problem. It can cost a lot for a potential buyer to do all the due diligence necessary to make an investment in your business. Purchasers could be reluctant to negotiate and spend the money on lawyers, accountants, and so on if there's a chance the vendor's other shareholders, cost-sharing associates, or partner(s) will exercise their right of first refusal. In addition, purchasers might not want to waste time waiting around for your fellow shareholders, cost-sharing associates, or partner(s) to make up their minds.

Our recommendation is to have your agreements modified to provide all parties with greater flexibility. The agreement could state that the vendor has to get a professional valuation that is representative of fair market value (FMV). The business should then be offered to the vendor's fellow shareholders, cost-sharing associates or partner(s) for that FMV price. If they decide not to buy after a reasonable period of time, say thirty to sixty days, then they should sign off and leave you free to sell your interest to whomever you choose. In this case, one of the concerns many groups have is, what if you sell to someone the other parties to the arrangement don't like or can't get along with on a business or professional level? To offer some comfort, the agreement can provide that the person you sell to must be qualified and have a good reputation. It is also possible to add wording to the effect that the other shareholders, cost-sharing associates, or partner(s) must approve of the purchaser and that such approval cannot be unreasonably withheld. Your lawyer should be able to help you with the appropriate wording. Just explain what you would like in plain language. It will be your lawyer's job to turn what you say into suitable "legalese."

Investment Strategies

Your investment strategies should be designed to maintain the integrity of your capital and grow in accordance with the assumptions you used regarding their growth. An important point to remember is that when it comes to investments, no one knows what the future will bring. The only aspect about investing that you can control with any certainty is risk. (See Investment Strategies chapter.)

Tax Planning

It's vital that you have the proper tax planning in place. This book contains a chapter on tax strategies that covers alternatives that have been employed successfully in other business situations. The idea of this chapter is not to make you a tax expert. Rather, this information should allow you to have meaningful discussions with the financial members of your transition advisory team. There's no point in paying extra tax if you don't have to, provided that your tax strategies aren't too extreme. Stick to proven mainstream strategies and stay away from tax-sheltered investments and insurance products unless they've been thoroughly reviewed by a fee-for-service expert who has no conflicts of interest.

Monitoring Your Progress

We recommend that you monitor your progress regularly and update your transition strategies at least every twelve months. Ideally, consider quarterly reviews for monitoring purposes. At the end of each quarter, simply set aside a little time to do your review. You'll want to know if the business (production, expenses, and profitability) is performing according to expectations, your spending is in line with your assumptions, and your investment portfolio is producing the results you require.

At the end of the year, review what has happened over the previous twelve-month period with your advisory team and consider what might be reasonably expected to change over the next twelve months. Typical changes might include:

- an increase in your cost structure—can you pass it on to the customers, clients, or patients or do you have to absorb all or most of the impact?
- a staff change, particularly if it's a key person in your organization;
- regulatory changes such as a change in tax legislation or the regulations affecting your profession or industry;
- the economic or investment outlook;
- your transition goals;
- your personal circumstances and/or needs.

A review of actual performance and consideration of changes that will occur in the next twelve-month period will help you put a meaningful new plan in place for the coming year.

The Non-Financial Implications of Your Transition

The non-financial implications of your transition were dealt with in considerable detail in chapter one, Step Ten, but its importance bears some repetition. Moving from a busy robust enterprise to retirement is more than the successful disposition of your business and achieving financial stability. It's a question of "What is going to bring fulfillment for the rest of my life?" Our experience has been that the most successful retired business people are those who planned with the same good sense and enthusiastic approach they used to build their career or business. They had a goal and a plan to participate in some meaningful activity that happily contributes to using up a good deal of the more than two thousand extra hours a year now at their disposal. After all, many find there is only so much golf, travelling, or sitting in the sun they can do before life becomes a dull routine. The most successful retirees don't retire from something. In fact, they retire *to* something!

The next three chapters deal specifically with:
• Wealth Management strategies,
• Wealth Creation strategies (for when your assessments indicate that you do have the Discretionary Cash Flow to build the required wealth), and
• Wealth Creation for when there is an identified Resource Gap.

You might find it interesting to read each of these chapters in detail. Or, in the interest of saving time, you could review in depth only the chapter(s) that specifically apply to your unique situation.

Chapter Five
Financial Independence and Transition Strategies – Wealth Management

This chapter will help those who:
- **Do have sufficient investable assets for relative financial security,**
- **Have a good understanding of their Current Position, and**
- **Have clearly defined and properly quantified long-term retirement goals.**

If you've determined that you have the required capital today or have an asset base that, if left invested until your transition could grow to the level needed for your relative financial security, congratulations! That's quite an accomplishment in today's world and it must be satisfying to recognize that you're in such a good financial position. The principal focus of transition and retirement strategies for you can be summed up with the term *Wealth Management*. To maintain this desirable financial position will take effort.

McNulty's Coaching Advice
Have your Current Position calculations and projections checked and double-checked by the financial members of your transition advisory team!

It's important that you ensure no errors were made in arriving at the figures for your Current Position. It's also critical to ensure that the assumptions used by you and your team were reasonable. Let us refer to a case from our files to illustrate the importance of this point.

Case Study

A new client came into our office a number of years ago, who, in addition to operating his business, also owned an equity position in another enterprise. This other firm was a relatively new business that appeared to have great potential. At the time, he was approximately eight years away from his intended transition date. In discussing his Current Position, he felt strongly about the future value of this outside company. The assumptions he used for the growth of this asset over the next eight years and his expectations with respect to selling the company some day were extremely aggressive. My client's role in this new venture was to supply investment capital. He wasn't actively involved in the day-to-day running of the company.

The question that immediately came to mind was whether or not it was reasonable to use aggressive assumptions about this operating company in planning for his transition. Statistics show that the success rate of new ventures is not good. It is not uncommon, however, for a start-up company to present a rosy outlook, especially to those who are capable of investing much needed capital. Unfortunately, the sad reality is that a high percentage of such opportunities are not even in existence after ten years. As it happened, using very aggressive assumptions about the success of this company indicated that this client would have virtually no need for any additional savings to meet his transition goals. On the other hand, when the success of a transition plan is heavily dependent on the success of one asset for which aggressive assumptions are being used, caution is well advised. When we removed the startup from the equation, there was a significant shortfall between what would be needed upon retirement and the expected growth of his other assets. Our advice was to proceed with a Wealth Creation plan designed to build the required capital for his transition goals for the first few years.

There are just too many unknowns associated with new companies to have such an important matter as your transition heavily dependent on its successful outcome. In this case, if the investment in the company didn't work out, there wouldn't be a problem. If the company does turn out to be a success, it would be a bonus and we could make adjustments to our figures.

McNulty's Coaching Advice

As a general guideline, when it comes to assumptions, err on the conservative side.

There's a form of analysis called probability analysis that you might find useful in determining how realistic your assumptions are. The idea is to vary assumptions, such as inflation rates, investment returns, taxation, and other key factors to measure the probability of the projected outcome turning out as anticipated. Ask a financial member of your transition team to perform this type of analysis, particularly if you're within a few years of your intended full transition date. It will help to provide you with confidence in your strategies. Incidentally, there are computer programs available (your advisor will likely have one) that can facilitate such an analysis.

Are You Making Assumptions About the Sale of Your Business?

If your planning relies on selling the business for a specific amount, and if you have not already done so, get a valuation from a creditable valuator (who should be considered part of your transition advisory team). Assuming your valuation confirms the value you have used in your analysis, the focus between now and your transition date, as it relates to the business, must be on managing its value to achieve that end. If you've been thinking about slowing down as you get closer to your transition date, check with your valuator first to make sure you fully understand the impact this decision could have on its potential resale value.

Tax planning is another reason to invest in a professional valuation. Many business owners who count on the sale of their enterprise to help fund their transition goals often don't have a clear idea of the tax implications of the final sale. A professional valuation will break down the allocation of goodwill, equipment, leaseholds, and supplies. If you are incorporated, it will also consider the impact of selling shares versus assets on the potential price. This is vital information that the financial members of your advisory team will need. A review of planning alternatives when selling the business can be seen in chapter eight.

Would You Like to Try One of the Partial Transition Variations?

This is an option well worth considering for those who have the required financial resources today to sufficiently meet their transition vision. You might have heard about potential problems with either grooming an existing employee or associate or bringing one in to acquire an equity interest in your business. While there are no guarantees, there are steps you can take that can help to improve the odds of a favourable outcome. First, we recommend that you define exactly what characteristics you want in a potential partner or shareholder. In other words, create a profile of the ideal candidate.

Next, consider how you will integrate this person into your business and the new role they will assume. Typically in a partial transition, a potential purchaser of a portion of your business will either be an existing employee or associate or someone specifically brought in with the understanding that they will buy in. In either case, we strongly recommend that you establish a trial period during which you simulate the experience of having them as a partner or shareholder. For example, establish them in the role you think would be appropriate if the plan is a success (which you have defined in advance). Delegate the actual responsibility and authority they will need to carry it out. Part of your job will then be to act as a mentor and also to monitor closely how well they do. If possible, you might want to seek the advice and input of other trusted members of your staff. We would also strongly recommend that you document the arrangement legally.

Among other things, the agreement should define the trial period and the fact that you have sole discretion to terminate the relationship without cause or explanation. This agreement should also contain details on what the employee or associate will be buying, for how much, and how the enterprise will operate after the trial period. It should also give you the right that if the employee or associate were to invest right away, to buy them out for exactly the same amount that they invested. While there is a lot to think about in a situation such as this, the legal member of your transition team should be able to help you here. This agreement should be prepared in advance.

It is also recommended that you do a Kolbe test to provide you with information on your strengths and weaknesses and, among other things, with whom you might best work. Finding the right person, one who will fit into your organization, will be challenging. It's difficult, on the basis of a few hours of interviews, to gain real insight into someone's personality. Most people are on their best behaviour during such times. Have any potential candidate do one as well and compare their results with your own. Kolbe tests are useful to determine whether a candidate's personality is likely to complement your own. They aren't costly and can be accessed with a credit card through the Internet at www.kolbe.com. Myers-Briggs and Insight also offer similar types of tests, which can be useful in determining potential compatibility with yourself and your team.

Case Study: Wealth Management

"John" and "Tammy" live in Niagara Falls, Ontario, and have three children. Sandra is twenty-four, Brian is twenty-two, and Neil is nineteen. Sandra and Brian both have one more year of university to go, while Neil has three. John and Tammy currently pay $53,000 per year for their children's expenses.

John has been a sole proprietor for twenty-four years. He and his team have built a profitable consulting service in the high-tech field. While he has been successful over the years, he has recently obtained several very lucrative contracts. Tammy has worked in the business the entire time in various capacities and currently earns $26,000 per year. John is age fifty and Tammy is fifty-one. Both are in good health.

John and Tammy are now "empty nesters" and, as such, recently downsized their home. They now live in a home worth $1 million that has no mortgage. They also have a cottage in Muskoka that is worth $350,000 and is also mortgage free.

They have never had to live on a budget and are not sure what it costs them to live on a monthly basis. While they agree they need to confirm this number, they feel comfortable using $150,000 after tax per year.

They would like to be financially independent in five years. This is defined as the ability to work out of choice rather than necessity. According to a recent valuation by a business valuator, the value of John's business is $1 million dollars, and he expects to sell the business in five years.

Both John and Tammy describe themselves as conservative investors who rely on their advisor to manage the accounts.

John and Tammy have no stated estate objective. In other words, they do not plan on leaving a significant amount of money to a charity or to the kids. With this in mind, we are to review the current universal life policies that John currently holds, as the premiums are quite high and the structure is complicated.

The only other goal they have is to be prepared to pay for Sandra's wedding in three years, as she is in a serious relationship and is planning to get married.

Quantified Goals

Financial Independence Goal

Based on analysis and the assumptions used, in order to achieve full financial independence by age fifty-five there is no need to save any additional funds over and above RRSPs.

Assumptions:
- Retirement lifestyle costs of $150,000 in present-day spending power, which is based on their estimate of current monthly expenses (excluding income tax, kids, insurance, and savings) plus an allowance for automobiles and additional travel;
- A 7% return (4% over inflation) on their retirement portfolio;
- Current tax regulations;
- Lifespan to age ninety for both spouses;
- Inflation of 3%;

Wedding Savings

In order to pay for a $40,000 wedding in three years, analysis indicates that they need to save $15,000 per year. This is based on the assumption that wedding costs are increasing at a rate of 4% per year and the savings would only be earning 1% net after tax.

Starting Point

Having quantified goals, this is where John and Tammy are today in a financial sense. Strategies can then be built to take them from where they are today to where they want to go.

Cash Flow: Projection for Next Year

Inflow

John's income	$625,000
Tammy's income	$26,000
Total Inflows	**$651,000**

Expenses

Income tax estimate	$272,000
Lifestyle expenses	$150,000
Kids' costs	$53,000
RRSP/Pension contributions	$21,180
Total Expenses	**$496,180**

Surplus (Deficit)	**$154,820**

Net Worth: Current Year

Assets	John	Tammy	Joint	Total
Cash in savings	$10,000			$10,000
JMS Consultants	$1,000,000			$1,000,000
Non-registered investments	$1,300,000	$300,000		$1,600,000
RRSPs	$475,000	$275,000		$750,000
Personal use assets	$875,000	$875,000		$1,750,000
Total Assets	**$3,660,000**	**$1,450,000**		**$5,110,000**

Liabilities

Total Liabilities	**$0**

Family Net Worth	**$5,110,000**

Planning Issues and Opportunities

An analysis of John and Tammy's current financial circumstances relative to their long-term objectives indicates that they are now financially independent. In other words, it is not necessary to come up with strategies which will focus their resources on building the financial security they will need in the future or to create wealth. Rather, their emphasis would be on capital preservation and strategies to enhance their already rosy outlook. To that end they may want to consider:

• Strategies to balance assets between Tammy and John. At the moment, investment assets are too heavily weighted in John's name. That situation can result in higher taxes than necessary in the post-transition stage of their lives.

• Current tax planning such as incorporation and income-splitting opportunities.

• Organizing the portfolio with a primary objective of preservation of capital.

Investment Strategy for Retirement Capital
The current asset class breakdown is as follows:

Portfolio Worksheet

Asset Class	Market Value	% Portfolio
Cash Equivalents	$350,000	15%
Fixed Income	$350,000	15%
Real Estate	$50,000	2%
Canadian Equities	$1,000,000	43%
International Equities	$500,000	21%
US Equities	$100,000	4%
Specialty Equities	$0	
Alternative Investments	$0	
Total expenses	**$2,350,000**	**100%**

The required rate of return on the investments, which will complement John and Tammy's long-term plan, is 7% (4%

over inflation). The current portfolio appears to be designed for growth. Equities account for 70% of the portfolio, which makes for a volatile asset base. Given historic risk and return measures for each asset class, there is a high probability over the next year in the range between 29% and -14%. This is a wide range. In addition, they do not need to be exposed to this much volatility. The higher the potential return, the higher the risk. Their time horizon is only five years to retirement at which point they will want to start living off the portfolio. As long as they do not lose money, the analysis indicates John and Tammy will be fine. A more appropriate portfolio would be organized so that the range of return that was likely in any one year would be much narrower.

Cash Flow Confirmation

An important estimate used in the plan is the retirement lifestyle estimate of $150,000 after tax, indexed for inflation. Most successful people do not have a very good idea of what it costs them to live every month. It would be prudent therefore over the next year or so, using the Banking by Objectives program, to confirm that this figure is adequate to meet their anticipated retirement spending needs.

Chapter Six
Financial Independence
and Transition Strategies –
Wealth Creation

This chapter will help those who:
- **Have a good understanding of their Current Position,**
- **Have clearly defined and properly quantified long-term retirement goals, and**
- **Don't currently have enough net free investment capital to meet retirement goals, but do have Discretionary Cash Flow available to set aside funds identified as the amount necessary to build the required pool of retirement capital.**

After assessing what your financial situation is today (your Current Position) relative to your clearly defined goals, you'll fall into one of the three categories covered in the introduction to transition strategies in chapter four. What follows in this chapter is appropriate for those whose situation is best described by the second category: you do not have enough net free capital, if invested today, to expect that it would grow to a level sufficient to finance your retirement. However, your analysis indicates that you do have the uncommitted Cash Flow to meet the identified savings need.

This uncommitted Cash Flow is considered Discretionary Cash. It represents after-tax income that you do not need to finance your lifestyle. At this point, you might be asking, "If I have all this cash left over each year, where did it go?" Well, unless you have some system in place to manage it, this cash tends to be spent on secondary priorities or on impulse. When you look back, it's almost like the cash evaporated because when money is spent in this manner it's hard to remember where it went.

Discretionary Cash Flow is one of the most strategically valuable financial resources you have. It can have a powerful impact on your financial security, level of financial stress, and freedom to live your life the way you want. Knowing this, we have experimented with various systems over the years to find the best one to effectively harness this potent resource. The end result is a system we call Banking by Objectives (BBO). It is easy to set up, simple to work with, and successful when used.

The BBO system was explained in chapter two. BBO is a very effective way to manage your Cash Flow and focus your Discretionary Cash resources on your most important objectives. In fact, we use it ourselves.

A Quick Note on Using Automatic BBO Systems

Many unincorporated businesses have operating lines of credit, and there's nothing wrong with having one: few businesses operate efficiently without borrowed funds. Typically, a line of credit operates as follows: deposits automatically decrease the amount owing and withdrawals (writing a cheque) increase it. If you have an operating line of credit in your business, it is important to make sure that the savings aren't coming from an increase in the amount owing from this business liability.

If you have a line of credit that's generally used within the business, we recommend that you do the transfers yourself. An Internet banking capability is perfect in these circumstances. If your assumptions are correct and you have the discretionary funds to meet your identified savings objective, there should be no increase in your debt obligations as a result of the BBO program!

On the other hand, if you find that the amount owing on your line of credit increases beyond normal use levels after setting up the BBO system, you might not have the Discretionary Cash you thought you did. In this case, you would want to review the reasons for the increase with the financial member of your transition advisory team. It might even be necessary to switch your strategies to the ones referred to in chapter seven, Wealth Creation—the Resource Gap.

Case Study

"Jim" and his wife, "Maryann," live in a medium-sized urban centre. Jim owns and operates a successful retail store that they purchased about twenty years ago. He operates as a proprietorship. He just turned fifty while Maryann is age forty-six. Both are in good health. They have one son who is at university in his second year of an arts program and another son who has not yet finished high school. Their second son, at this point, doesn't appear to be interested in going on to university. They feel he will likely attend the local community college.

Their goals are to educate their children, sell the store in ten years when Jim turns sixty, and retire. Jim and Maryann feel that they could finance a satisfying retirement lifestyle on what $75,000 after tax would buy today.

Now let's use their situation to look at some numbers. Their Current Position at the time that we first established his transition plan looked like the following:

Business

Gross revenue after cost of goods sold	$780,000
Less general and administrative expenses	$452,400
Less salary to Maryann	$ 42,000
Net Income	$285,600

Personal Income

Jim	$285,600
Maryann	$ 42,000
Net Inflow of Funds	$327,600

Expenditures

Income tax (avg. rate = 36%)	$ 117,936
Personal living expense estimate	$ 90,000
Principal on business debt	$ 22,000
Debt service on cottage mortgage	$ 6,395
University costs for son	$ 15,000
RRSPs	$ 24,060
Total Expenditures	**$ 275,391**
Surplus (Deficit)	**$ 52,209**

Net Worth

Assets

Cash or near cash	$ 22,000
Business value (after tax)	$350,000
RRSPs	$575,000
Non-Registered Investments	$ 85,000
RESPs	$ 65,000
House	$450,000
Cottage	$170,000
Cars	$ 45,000
Household effects	$120,000
Total Assets	**$1,882,000**

Liabilities

Business line of credit	$ 40,000
Business renovation loan	$180,000
Cottage mortgage	$ 48,000
Total Liabilities	**$268,000**

Net Worth	**$1,614,000**

Net assets that could currently be devoted towards retirement income are:
• The business less an allowance for selling and legal costs of say $40,000 and related debt of $220,000 for a net of $90,000;
• RRSPs of $575,000; and
• The non-registered portfolio of $85,000.
• This would bring the total to $750,000.

Working with the financial members of their advisory team, Jim and Maryann have determined that they have a savings need, in addition to regular RRSP contributions, of $44,999 (or $3,749.92 per month) to meet their transition objective.

According to the assessment of their Current Position, they have Discretionary Cash of $52,209 (or about $4,350 per month). Their savings objectives are therefore realistically attainable. In fact, that was the case in the actual situation from our files. There is one other benefit that is worth noting: Jim and Maryann should have a surplus after setting aside the funds for their savings goal of $7,210. That's about $600 per month. Knowing this figure has helped them manage their income and expenses because they understand how much they can afford to spend on secondary priorities or impulse items.

Jim and Maryann's BBO system was set up on a priority basis as follows:

1. Personal Living Account (with Overdraft Protection)

Two deposits of $3,750 each were made from the business account every month, one on the 1st of the month and the other on the 15th. At the end of each month, an additional deposit of $532.92 was made to this account for payment of the cottage mortgage. From this account, all other personal expenses were paid, including credit-card payments.

2. The Tax Account

Assuming funds were available at the end of the month, a deposit was made of the sum needed to make the required quarterly tax remittance on the 15th. In this case, we only have to be concerned about Jim's income tax because his wife's tax is remitted through source deductions. The amount to be deposited was $8,500 per month.

3. The Education Funding Account

While their education costs are estimated to be $15,000 annually, the monthly demand for money can fluctuate greatly. Jim deposited $1,250 per month to track these costs. However, when tuition has to be paid or books purchased (not to mention those calls from their son explaining all the excellent and logical reasons why his living allowance did not last!), they sometimes have to pre-fund this account. When that happens, the funds come from their cash reserve, net Discretionary Cash after savings for financial independence, or, if necessary, from a personal line of credit they have for such emergencies. From that point, all available funds that would have accumulated from the $1,250 per month deposits are used to repay the funds taken from their cash reserves or the line of credit.

4. The Financial Independence Savings Account

Jim and Maryann decided to deposit into this account every month a savings amount rounded to $3,800. Each quarter, provided the funds are not needed for an emergency, a decision is made as to how to invest these accumulated savings ($11,400) as part of their long-term investment strategy (see chapter nine for investment strategies).

5. The RRSP Account

Jim and Maryann set aside, provided the funds are available, $2,005 per month so that they will have the necessary cash when it comes time to make their annual RRSP contribution. They know they get the best returns from their RRSPs by making their deposits early, at the beginning of the year, rather than during the following February for the year that has just past. These deposits, therefore, fund an advance contribution to the RRSP each year.

6. Discretionary Spending Account

The remaining Discretionary Cash estimate of $551 per month is deposited to this account when it is available. Note that the principal payments on the business debt are paid through the business accounts.

Monitoring Your BBO System

Monitoring your system is important because assumptions don't always work as expected. Things such as tax laws, inflation, actual investment returns (or, heaven forbid, investment losses) etc., will impact your objective. One of the great things about the BBO money management system is that it facilitates monitoring. It's really a great feedback system without all the hassles of a paper or computer budget. A simple review of your various bank accounts will tell you whether you're "on plan" or not.

If everything is working properly, you'll be able to see your results and experience the satisfaction that comes with being in control of your finances. On the other hand, if at the end of a particular fiscal quarter the BBO system hasn't worked as anticipated, you can make modifications in a timely manner.

What if the program is not working as planned? We all know that the monthly inflows and outflows of cash from a business can fluctuate quite dramatically. Some months are shorter than others and sometimes you can have a great month. That's why deposits to the BBO must be prioritized. In any given month when there is not enough cash available to make all the planned deposits, the funds that are available must be used for the most important purpose. Over the course of any given quarter, the averages should generally be equal to your plan.

McNulty's Coaching Advice

Although rare, it can happen that your Cash Flow turns out to be higher than expected. In this case, you would see either your operating line of credit decrease or a buildup of funds in your business account. We recommend that these funds be set aside but not touched until you are sure they are not going to be needed.

When the BBO system doesn't work, it's due to one of three reasons:

1. It's possible there was a human error, either on your part or, as often occurs, on the part of the bank.
2. Your inflow of cash was lower than anticipated.
3. Your outflow in terms of business or personal expenditures was higher than anticipated.

Depending on the reasons noted above, you might have to adapt your savings plan for the year. It's important to consider whether or not the money will be available to make up the deficit by the end of the year. If the answer is no, the best advice is to go back to the proverbial drawing board and do some recalculating.

The example of John and Maryann illustrates how the

Wealth Creation program would work in an unincorporated business. If you are in a partnership, the format is not that much different. In this situation, you treat your share of net revenue as your income just as our friend Jim here did by taking the equivalent partnership draw.

If your business is incorporated, the basic concept still applies. There are some additional complexities however. Of course, rather than all net revenue after expenses falling into your hands, from a practical and tax viewpoint, the funds that are earned are earned by the company. Your personal income would then come out by way of salary, bonuses, and/or dividends. There are also additional strategies you might consider that could save you some tax, such as using a trust to fund expenses for the kids (see chapter eight).

One decision you will have to make if you are incorporated is whether to save the funds you have identified for your transition and retirement either in the company or personally. Corporations that are subject to the small-business deduction limit can have a lower average tax rate than you do personally. If you own 100% of the shares of the company, you may decide not to pay out the funds you need for personal savings if your average tax rate exceeds that which the company will have to pay. Instead, you might want to consider saving the funds in the corporate environment; doing so can result in a worthwhile deferral of some tax. If you intend to keep the company in place on transition (the company would sell assets instead of shares), then it would be important to consider the fact that there will be a tax cost when the funds are withdrawn during retirement. Additional annual savings might be necessary to compensate for this fact. This would not be an option, in our view, if there are other arm's-length shareholders in the company, unless your shares are owned by a holding company that would allow you to pass your share of after-tax profits up to it. There are a lot of alternatives that can be used to deal with such corporate surpluses, such as Retirement Compensation Arrangements, individual pension plans, and so on. For a more in-depth discussion, see chapter eight. Also, due to the potential complexity, we strongly advise you to explore your alternatives with the tax professional member of your transition team.

Whether you are incorporated, a member of a partnership, or own a proprietorship, you should find the BBO system one of the easiest cash management systems available to work with. It's a management-by-exception system that gives you control of this important aspect of your personal finances.

Updating Your BBO

At the end of twelve months, it's time to create a new savings plan for the coming year. This review process helps to ensure that your planning and strategies remain current and meaningful. Timing is important. Establish well in advance the time to do this update with the appropriate members of your advisory team and make sure this time commitment is noted in your office schedule. To make sure you're all working on the same schedule, the steps are as follows:

- Quantify your goals again, taking into account your progress over the last year and the fact you're now one year older.
- Work out what the new savings figure needs to be, given the results you had in the past year combined with your outlook for the coming year.

Repeating this process every year will help you to adjust to changes that could affect your financial security, such as inflation, tax regulation, business or practice income, investment returns, and the economic outlook.

In summary, it's our hope that this extensive case study shows that the best way to capture the required portion of Discretionary Cash is to put in place a system that's easy to work with and simple to monitor.

Case Study: Wealth Creation

"David" and "Jackie" live in Toronto, Ontario, and are the parents of two wonderful children, Jonathan, age fourteen and Tanya, age eleven. David is the owner/operator of an unincorporated business XYZ Consultants. Jackie has worked for XYZ earning $26,000 per year since it opened ten years ago. Jackie also works part-time as a teacher earning $25,000 per year (no pension).

Their principal residence is estimated at being worth $750,000 and is in Jackie's name. Jackie and David have worked hard their entire lives and have recently celebrated becoming totally debt-free with the final payment of their mortgage.

David is now age forty-four and Jackie is forty-three. They would like to be financially independent by the time David turns fifty-five. The nature of David's consulting business makes it unlikely that it will sell. He has a great deal of professional goodwill but no real commercially transferable goodwill. In other words, there will probably be no proceeds from the sale of the business to go towards their financial independence plan. As such, all of the funding required to meet their objectives will have to come from the income generated in the business.

Another objective that David and Jackie have is that they would like to be in a position to pay for an undergraduate degree (four-year degree) for each child.

Summary of Objectives

- To achieve financial independence by the time David turns fifty-five. Financial independence is defined as the ability to work out of choice rather than necessity. The objective would be to maintain their current personal lifestyle spending level after tax, indexed for inflation until Jackie turns ninety.
- To save the funds necessary to pay for an undergraduate degree for each child.

Quantified Goals

Financial Independence Goal

At present, it is estimated that Jackie and David could finance a very acceptable retirement lifestyle for $100,000 per year after tax. This figure was arrived at by reviewing current monthly expenses (excluding income tax, support for the kids, insurance, and savings) plus adding an allowance for periodic expenses such as replacement of automobiles. Based on an analysis by their advisory team employing assumptions considered reasonable by David and Jackie, they would need to save $72,500 of tax-paid capital per year for the next eleven years plus RRSPs to finance this objective.

Education Savings Goal

Jonathan, age fourteen, will begin his post-secondary education in four years. As there is currently no money set aside to fund this degree, the annual required savings is $16,000 after tax.

Tanya is eleven and will begin her post-secondary education in seven years. To pay for her undergraduate degree, required annual savings are $9,800 after tax.

Each calculation assumes a conservative investment return and education costs indexed by 4%.

Starting Point

Having quantified their goals, it is now necessary to determine where they are today in a financial sense. Strategies can then be established using the foundation of a thorough understanding of what their financial starting point is, to get them from where they are right now to where they want to be in the future.

Cash Flow: Current Year

Inflow

David's income	$300,000
Jackie's XYZ salary	$26,000
Jackie's teaching income	$25,000
Total Inflows	**$351,000**

Expenses

Income taxes*	$123,449
Lifestyle expenses	$100,000
Kids' costs	$3,500
RRSP contributions	$25,680
Total Expenses	**$252,629**
Surplus (Deficit)	**$98,371**

*Income tax projection based on 2005 applicable deductions, taxes, and credits.

Net Worth: Current Year

	David	Jackie	Joint	Total
Assets				
Cash in savings	$10,000			$10,000
Non-Registered Investments				
RRSPs	$225,000	$75,000		$300,000
Personal Use Assets	$750,000	$250,000		$1,000,000
Total Assets				**$1,310,000**
Liabilities				**$ 0**
Net Worth				**$1,310,000**

Planning Issues and Opportunities

Wealth Creation

Based on an analysis of their current financial position, it appears David and Jackie have $98,371 per year of Discretionary Cash Flow available for goal funding. Required saving for education is $25,800 and for their financial independence is $72,500 for a total of $98,300. It would therefore seem that they have the available Discretionary Cash Flow to meet their most important objectives. Having the funds and actually creating the required wealth is not necessarily the same thing. To reach their objective, they and their advisory team should consider:

- Incorporation, perhaps with Jackie and a trust for the kids owning shares, to take advantage of the potential tax-deferral and income-splitting benefits;
- Establishing a monthly financial independence savings objective, either within the corporation if that is their decision or outside of it so that the identified funds are set aside automatically (note: if they decide to incorporate and save the money in the corporate environment, a larger savings figure will have to be established to recognize the fact that some tax will be payable on withdrawal. The quantified savings objective of $72,500 is based on tax-paid capital).
- Opening a Registered Educational Savings Plan (RESP) for both kids and contributing the maximum of $4,000 for each. This should also qualify them for the Canada Education Savings Grant (CESG). A system to save the balance of the required $17,800 automatically should then be established. If they decide to incorporate with a trust for the kids owning some shares, funds could be accumulated within the company until they reach the age of eighteen to avoid the "kiddie tax." Also, if funds are saved within the corporation in this manner, no adjustment is necessary to the required savings amount

as there should be no tax cost for passing the amount of dividends that will be necessary through the trust to the kids (once they are eighteen) because of their personal tax credits and the dividend tax credit.

- Part of their long-term financial independence strategies should be balancing the investment assets between David and Jackie to facilitate tax planning in the post-transition period.
- Their plan should be monitored quarterly and updated annually to make sure they stay on track and accomplish their objectives.

Chapter Seven
Financial Independence
and Transition Strategies –
Wealth Creation –
The Resource Gap

This chapter will help those who:
- **Have a good understanding of their Current Position,**
- **Have clearly defined and properly quantified long-term retirement goals, and**
- **Do have a Resource Gap, meaning that they don't have the current resources or the required Discretionary Cash to meet their goals.**

It is said that knowing you have a problem is the first step in solving it. Being aware of a Resource Gap can empower you to take action and gain control of your financial affairs. By doing so now, you won't have any nasty surprises down the road and you can build toward the future that's right for you and your family. So let's get started! There are fundamentally three options you can choose from to deal with your Resource Gap: increase your inflow, decrease your outflow, and/or change your goals.

1. Increase Your Inflow

When facing a Resource Gap, experience has shown that increasing inflow is by far the most preferable and successful of the three options—that's provided it can be done without working yourself to death! Inflow is the net Cash Flow available from your business after tax, whether you're incorporated or not. There are basically three ways to do this. You can increase revenue, decrease expenses, or both. In practice, we have found the best results come from a combination of these strategies depending on your circumstances. If this is your preferred alternative, it is important to properly define just how much of an increase you will need.

Let's consider a Resource Gap example for a proprietorship or professional practice. Assume that with the help of your transition advisory team, you have determined it necessary to set aside $35,000 per year, in addition to your RRSP contributions, to reach your transition goals. Suppose it's apparent from your Current Position that at this point in time you only have $15,000 of Discretionary Cash available. The net result is a Resource Gap of $20,000 after tax.

Think of this process as a bottom-up exercise. Unfortunately, the actual figure you need to obtain is not $20,000. Why? Because to that $20,000 you must first add tax. In this case, as a proprietor, this additional money will most likely be coming in, for tax purposes, at the top marginal tax rate. In Ontario, the top rate in 2005 was approximately 46%. (In this example, we have used a 2005 tax rate from only one province. To be meaningful, you will have to adapt the example to the province where you live and the year the calculation was prepared.) For the purpose of this exercise, let us assume that about 54¢ out of every extra dollar you make can be applied to your Resource Gap. If you take your objective of $20,000 and divide it by 54%, the answer gives you the pre-tax incremental amount of $37,037 ($20,000/.54) that you need to bring into income. But you're not there yet. This figure, to be of value in a strategic planning sense, still needs greater definition. You must also answer the question of how much additional variable overhead you'll have to incur to generate this incremental pretax income. If you sell a product rather than provide a service, work out what your gross profit is per unit (if that is appropriate in your business) and deduct applicable variable expenses to determine the dollar volume you are going to need to meet your transition objective.

Variable Overheads or Expenses

Variable overheads or expenses are an important consideration when you're trying to identify what additional income must be brought in to reach your objectives. These are the expenses that increase or decrease with the ebb and flow of revenue. When identifying the target amount that you need to earn, ask yourself what you'll have to spend to generate this additional revenue. Obvious examples might be supplies, the cost of goods sold, shipping costs, sales commissions, promotional expenses, or additional manufacturing costs depending on the type of business you are in.

You might simply know off the top of your head what expenses are variable. If you don't, or if you need a reference source to make sure you've identified all variable expenses, we'd recommend looking at your Profit and Loss Statements (sometimes referred to as income statements). Typically, your accountant, as part of your annual financial statements, prepares Profit and Loss Statements. They're the best source for information like this. Simply assemble statements that cover a few years. Calculate the percentages that each expense item represents of that year's gross revenue. Identifying what expenses increased or decreased (other than normal inflationary increments) with a corresponding increase or decrease in that gross revenue number will help you identify all your variable costs.

For the purposes of our example, assume that your variable costs work out to be 20%. In other words, out of every dollar of extra revenue (after cost of goods sold if you sell a product as opposed to a service), 80¢ should drop to your bottom line. Going back to the pre-tax figure, we worked out to arrive at an after-tax sum of $20,000, divide $37,037 by 80% ($37,037/.80). According to our calculations, that would be $46,296.25 per year.

McNulty's Coaching Advice

It's always prudent to plan for contingencies, so round off your objective amount to the next highest $10,000. In this case, we are talking about $50,000 of additional revenue to produce that $20,000 needed to make up the Resource Gap.

Any annual figure that you calculate is likely to be a big number (such as the $50,000 in the above example). It might be a little intimidating. The secret is to break down such large sums into workable bites. For example, assume you are a professional working 230 days per year. If we go back to our figure of $50,000 and divide it by 230, you would only have to earn an additional $217.39 per day in incremental production to meet your objective. Alternately, if we assume you are in the retail business, by understanding your gross profit after cost of goods sold, you should be in a position to break down this same $50,000 into what you must do in the way of daily incremental sales to meet your objective. When you think in terms of $50,000, it's difficult to come up with workable strategies for such a big number. That's probably because we don't work on a yearly basis. Any annual accomplishment is likely the result of daily actions. Once you've worked out what you need on a daily basis, it's a lot easier to come up with realistic strategies, which brings us to the next point.

After properly defining what you would need to produce to sufficiently increase your inflow, the next question you must answer is, can it be done and how? There's a basic rule when it comes to establishing strategies: they should be realistically attainable. Can you develop strategies to bring in an additional $218 per day (using the proprietorship example above)?

In our experience, every business, profession, and industry has "best practices" that could be used to increase your revenue or sales to the desired level. You will have to decide which alternative or group of alternatives is best for you. Some alternatives will be more complex and expensive than others, so list them all and choose the simplest and least expensive first, unless you're concerned that they won't be effective. You might even want to hire an expert in your field to help you develop your strategies. One option you can look into is making use of any government programs that are available to you. There are programs whereby you can access retired executives with expertise in a wide variety of disciplines such as business plan preparation, marketing, or sales management in a very cost-effective manner. Whatever avenue you take when seeking such advice, be very specific about what you want from the consultant's engagement because they can be expensive. Without direction, their strategies can also involve more disruption than your circumstances actually require. Tell them the exact amount of additional gross revenue you need, and remember, to be successful, the engagement must also produce enough additional revenue to pay their fee. It's also important to have a monitoring process to keep track of their progress and expenses.

Another Strategy for Increasing Your Bottom Line

In the preceding paragraphs, we suggested that you assemble several years of Profit and Loss Statements. Use them to calculate what percentage each category of expense represents in terms of gross revenue and then compare these figures to industry averages. This information is often available through trade or professional associations. Your accountant might also be a good source for this kind of information. Are any of your costs too high relative to industry or profession averages? If it appears your expenses are abnormally high relative to the profession or industry as a whole, discuss strategies for reducing them with your transition advisory team. It can very often be worth the exercise. When you reduce your expenses as opposed to increasing your revenue, the money usually drops right to the bottom line since you don't have to factor in various incremental costs as you do when revenue is increased.

We can recall working with a professional whose practice had slowed down a little. The problem was that while his gross revenue declined, his fixed expenses (rent, telephone, staff, and so on) didn't change. As a result, his personal income was drastically reduced. The solution was to move another practitioner into his office to share space and fixed expenses. This was done together with a change in calendar management so that the client hardly ever saw his cost-sharing colleague. Both practices enjoyed a significant increase in their bottom line and the client was able to cover his Resource Gap very nicely. While opportunities to decrease fixed business expenses are not always easy to identify, the possibility shouldn't be ignored.

Considerations for Partnerships and Corporations

If you're in a full partnership, it can be difficult to increase your individual income. The most common revenue-sharing we are familiar with are as follows:

- Partners simply share in the profits of the partnership on a proportional basis. In this case, they generally take an agreed upon draw to support their lifestyle needs during the periods between the distribution of profits.
- The net partnership profits are shared relative to each individual's contribution to revenue. Once again, an agreed upon draw is taken to support lifestyle in the periods between when profits are distributed.

- The formula entitles them to a percentage of their own personal income production and the rest goes into a common account to pay expenses, after which the remainder is split among all partners.

No matter what the formula is for your partnership, if you find you have a Resource Gap to deal with, the partnership model makes increasing inflow more complicated. For example, if you increase your personal production and your other partner(s) do not, then only part of that incremental revenue will fall into your hands (you might, however, get voted partner of the year by your colleagues). In a partnership, either all partners agree that they'll work to increase the bottom line or you might need to find another way to earn the additional required revenue.

Based on whatever partnership formula your group works under, identify what you need to produce to address your Resource Gap via an increase in inflow. Talk to your partners about it. If they are willing to adopt a business plan that will result in the incremental income you need, all is well and good. On the other hand, if they are not receptive, you might not have a lot of alternatives, depending on your circumstances. If you aren't able to increase income, you could be forced to move on to the other two options: decreasing your outflow or changing your goals.

If you operate under a corporate structure where you own or control 100% of the shares in the company, the fundamentals of increasing inflow are very similar to a proprietorship. However, while you control how the money will be paid out, the corporation is a separate entity under the law. So rather than an increase in net income falling directly into your hands, for tax and distribution purposes, some additional decision making will have to be done. For example, should the money be paid out as incremental salary, dividends, or bonuses? Alternately, what about saving the funds needed to bridge the Resource Gap in the company itself? We would recommend that you work closely with the financial members of your advisory team to determine the best option for you.

If your business is structured as a corporation where you do not own all of the shares, then you might find yourself faced with a situation similar to that of a partnership as described above.

McNulty's Coaching Advice
Set up a system such as Banking by Objectives (chapter two) to make sure funds are available for their intended purpose. It's all too easy when funds are mixed in the general pool of family monies to make an impulse decision to expend these additional resources. Set the money aside to fund your transition and other important priorities first, and then you can spend the rest however you want.

2. Decrease Your Outflow
By way of general comment, let us say that in over twenty-five years of working with independent business people, we have found that the least effective alternative when dealing with a Resource Gap is to decrease personal lifestyle expenses. It just doesn't seem to work, and many times it causes strife within the family. Only in extreme cases, where no other alternatives exist, do we recommend reducing personal expenditures. That being the case, let's look at some ways that can be effective at reducing outflow.

Reorganizing Debt
No one likes debt, and this means people are often committed to amortization schedules that are too rapid. The argument tends to go, "I'll pay off my debts and then I'll save for retirement." The problem with this is that people lose one of the great benefits of investing: the power of compounding. Now, we're not suggesting that you shouldn't

pay off your debts; rather, it's one place to look at if you're trying to find the funds to meet a defined savings objective. Some actions to consider are:

• Consolidating loans,
• Taking a longer amortization period, and
• Arranging for deductible debts to be interest only so that all the principal can be applied to non-deductible debt.

If you are a proprietor with business debt, consider incorporation and paying it back from the corporate entity. While the interest on such debt is tax deductible, repayment of the principal is not. For example, if we assume for ease of calculation that the top marginal tax rate is 50%, paying back $1 of principal on your proprietorship's debt takes $2 of pre-tax income.

Corporations, on the other hand, generally qualify for the small business deduction. This means the corporation's tax rate (see chapter eight for more information) is much lower and there is more after-tax money to pay back the principal on a business loan. For example, assume the corporation has a tax rate of 20%. Rather than having to earn $2 pre-tax to pay back $1 of debt as mentioned above, you would only have to earn $1.20. That's a significant advantage! Be sure to discuss this alternative in detail with your transition advisory team—incorporation is not for everyone and it can be expensive.

Selling Redundant Assets

We once had a client who had a beautiful cottage that was worth a significant amount of money. Not only did it cost a great deal in terms of maintenance, property taxes, and operating costs, it also had a sizeable non-deductible mortgage on it. The client was forced to make a decision: did he and his spouse prefer to keep the cottage, in which case projections indicated he wouldn't be able to do a transition until his mid-sixties, or did they think it was more important to be in a position to do a full transition by his late fifties, their intended transition date? Decisions like these are always difficult. What it comes down to is prioritizing what's truly important to you. In this case, the client decided to keep the cottage and change his transition goal. Given their Resource Gap, the objective of a full transition by their late fifties was simply not practical.

Reducing Income Tax

This can be very complex. In chapter eight, we outline a number of tax strategies that we've seen in common use over the years while working with independent business owners. These strategies include:

• Income splitting
• Incorporation
• Setting up separate companies with separate family ownership
• Retirement Compensation Arrangements
• Other strategies helpful in reducing taxes payable in a given year and therefore your outflow

Once again, discuss these strategy options in detail with your transition advisory team to make sure they are appropriate for your circumstances.

Budgeting versus Using a Priority Spending System

If you decide to reduce your personal lifestyle expenditures, we'd recommend you work on a priority-spending format. This system works on a monthly basis where spending is related to the net Cash Flow generated by the unincorporated business, or integrated personal and corporate Cash Flow in the previous month. It has to be the previous month because you make spending decisions in real time but typically you don't have information on what's happening with income and expenses and the resulting available cash on a daily basis. The answer is to operate with a line of credit in the business and restrict your draws or salary from the company to what cash was available from the previous month so that you don't overspend.

With these funds, the first category of expenses that should be paid includes basic living expenses such as food, insurance, shelter, clothing, and transportation. Basic living expenses do not include any extras like entertainment or any form of discretionary spending. Basic in this case really means *basic*. Next, taxes and debt service, if any, are to be paid. So far, these are costs that you really must pay. From this point on, however, you have decisions to make.

Reducing your personal expenditures is all about trade-offs. What is your most important priority? If your priority is creating financial security for yourself that will allow you to achieve your long-term succession goals, then the next item that should be set aside is the sum you've identified as your savings objective. Once again, using BBO, set these monies aside in a separate account so that they're identified with their purpose. Any money left over after these expenses and priorities have been taken care of can then be spent.

3. Change Your Goals

If you can't increase inflow and if, after examining the various trade-offs involved with decreasing outflow, you decide this also isn't a good option, you must look at changing your objectives. The sooner you do this, the better. There are two general changes you can make that should have a dramatic impact on the Resource Gap you have identified:

- You can decide to retire later. This means you will have longer to accumulate the necessary resources and you will be living off your assets (as opposed to your earnings) for less time.
- You can plan on spending less when you retire.

If, after completing a full transition, you plan to live on $150,000 per year after tax, it would take substantially more retirement capital than say living on $75,000 per year after tax. When working with your transition team's financial members, don't forget that at some point you might have the option of reducing retirement spending while at the same time allowing your accumulated capital to grow. In general, most people don't spend the same way at age eighty as they did at age sixty. One important consideration to keep in mind, however, is that it costs a significant amount of money if there is a need in later years for assisted living or a retirement residence. You can, of course, buy insurance to protect yourself against such costs but it is expensive and if you already have a Resource Gap, it could exacerbate the problem.

Time Is of the Essence

Successfully dealing with a Resource Gap is possible. It just requires looking carefully at your priorities and your lifestyle. The important thing is to act now—even with the smallest step. The sooner you put measures into place to close up your Resource Gap, the sooner you'll feel better about your overall transition plans.

Case Study: The Resource Gap

"Brian" and "Laura" live in Mississauga, Ontario, and are the proud parents of Mark, Tim, and Andrea. Brian is age forty-eight and Laura is forty-seven. All three of their children are currently in university. Mark, twenty-two, is in his last year at Waterloo. Tim, nineteen, is in his second year at Western, while Andrea, eighteen, has just started her first year at Waterloo.

Since 1988, Brian has owned and operated ABC Incorporated. Brian's wife, Laura, has worked for the government for many years but did take some time off to raise the kids. Her total years of service is seventeen, and she's eligible for an indexed pension at age sixty-five (currently eligible for $11,000 per year).

Having three children in university at the same time has been quite costly for Laura and Brian. Fortunately, they've always been ardent savers and had the funds set aside to pay for undergraduate degrees for the three kids. Giving their children a "good start in life" has always been a top priority in their lives. Even with the kids in school, they continue to set money aside to assist them with expenses once they graduate.

Brian personally also owns the building that houses his business, ABC Incorporated. The building is worth $720,000 and has a mortgage of $350,000.

Brian and Laura have a lovely home in Mississauga that's now worth $675,000. They have a personal line of credit outstanding in the amount of $398,000 secured by the house.

Brian isn't sure what it costs him and his wife to maintain their lifestyle, but all their personal expenses are paid from one bank account. Brian deposits his net salary into this bank account and Laura deposits all of her after-tax income.

In addition to paying for their children's education, Brian and Laura have also purchased a $17,000 car for each of their kids. Each child also receives income from ABC Incorporated.

To see their kids have a good start in life, Brian and Laura are saving $150 per month for each child (they have done this since the kids were young) which can be spent on whatever the kids decide when they reach an appropriate age. It's important to them to continue this savings plan. While Brian and Laura maximize their pension and RRSP contributions every year, the only other savings that take place are within a universal life insurance policy on Brian's life. The current savings taking place in this policy are $15,000 per year less premium and policy costs.

Brian has some savings in ABC Incorporated but doesn't have a goal in mind for this money. It's simply money that has been left over after paying all the expenses that have accumulated over the years.

While Brian and Laura haven't spent much time thinking about financial independence and/or retirement, they both feel that they would like to be in a position to work out of choice rather than necessity by the time Brian reaches age fifty-five. This would include the sale of the business, which has been recently valued at $400,000.

Another goal is to acquire property to retire to on a lake. Brian and Laura would expect this property to cost $550,000.

Summary of Objectives

- To achieve financial independence by the time Brian turns fifty-five. Financial independence is defined as being able to maintain a lifestyle equal to what could be purchased today for $100,000 per year after tax with a lifespan expectation of age ninety for both Brian and Laura.
- To purchase a bungalow on the lake for $550,000 at age fifty-five.
- To continue to save $150 per month for each child until they each turn twenty-five.

Quantified Goals

Financial Independence Goal

Based on the analysis and the assumptions used, in order to achieve full financial independence by age fifty-five, we estimate it would be necessary for Brian and Laura to save $67,723 per year in tax-paid capital for the next eight years. We have assumed retirement lifestyle costs of $100,000, based on current monthly expenses (excluding income tax, kids, insurance, and savings) plus an allowance for automobiles. Furthermore, maximum RRSP/Pension contributions would need to be made by both Laura and Brian during this eight-year period.

In the analysis, an 8% return (5% after inflation) is assumed on the retirement portfolio. The sum of $300,000 has also been included as proceeds (after tax and selling costs) from the sale of the business and $400,000 in net after-tax proceeds from the sale of the building that houses the business.

Purchase of $550,000 Retirement Property

No funding is needed for this goal as their current plan to sell their residence to purchase the new home will take care of it. The proceeds from downsizing have not been taken into account at this point in the savings plan, as what will remain after moving, selling, and renovation expenses cannot yet be determined.

Providing the Kids with a Good Start in Life

The funding for the kids' education is now complete. The ongoing $150 per month of savings for them is currently taking place and will be complete prior to Laura and Brian turning fifty-five. As such, no further planning is necessary.

Starting Point

Having quantified their goals, it is now important to determine where they are today in a financial sense. Strategies can then be designed, based on this solid foundation.

Cash Flow: Current Year

Inflow

Brian's income	$129,182
Brian's net rental income	($20,880)
Laura's income	$62,390
Total Inflows	**$170,692**

Expenses

Income taxes	$37,417
Lifestyle expenses	$88,825
RRSP/Pension contributions	$27,500
Universal life insurance	$15,000
Savings for kids	$5,400
Principal on LOC	$11,963
Total expenses	**$186,105**

Surplus (Deficit)	**($15,413)**

Note:

The "lifestyle expenses" are based on the understanding that all of Laura's income is deposited into one account along with $3,300 from Brian's income.

RRSP contributions are assumed to be $16,500 for Brian and $11,000 for Laura based on last year's earned income.

Net rental income relates to the net losses on the building that houses ABC.

Net Worth: Current Year

Assets	Brian	Laura	Joint	Total
Cash in savings	$43,637	$10,000		$53,637
ABC, Inc.	$400,000			$400,000
Savings within ABC, Inc.	$96,778			$96,778
Office building	$720,000			$720,000
Real estate investments	$472,000			$472,000
Kids' investment assets			$64,288	$64,288
Universal life savings	$27,181			$27,181
Non-registered investments	$24,775			$24,775
RRSPs	$125,050	$57,085		$182,135
Personal Use Assets			$855,000	$855,000
Total Assets	**$1,909,421**	**$67,085**	**$919,288**	**$2,895,794**

Liabilities

Office Building Mortgage	$350,000			$350,000
Investment Real Estate Loans	$398,745			$398,745
Total Liabilities	**$748,745**			**$748,745**
Net Worth				**$2,147,049**

Planning Issues and Opportunities

The Resource Gap

To achieve financial independence, Brian and Laura need to maximize RRSP/Pension savings and save $67,723 after tax. While their Net Worth is good and RRSP/Pension savings are already taking place, there is a current personal Cash Flow deficit. This is even before the identified savings required of $67,723 per year to meet their financial independence goal. Further, they have non-deductible debt to deal with. While there is some saving taking place in the corporation, these funds will likely be needed in future years to pay for this personal Cash Flow deficit.

Brian and Laura need to:

• Set up the right team of advisors to help them address their needs.
• Prepare a Bottom-Up Business Plan and determine if it is possible either by increasing revenue in Brian's business or by decreasing business expenses and their personal expenses to deal with their Cash Flow deficit, non-deductible debt and the financial independence savings of $67,723.

If this is not possible, they must consider what changes they are prepared to undertake. For example, they might want to consider selling the office building, changing their goals, eliminating other expenses, or perhaps a combination of strategies.

The point here is that Brian and Laura, having quantified their goals and established their current financial position, can now explore proactive realistic strategies to address their future.

Chapter Eight
Tax Strategies for Financial Independence and Transition

This chapter will help you:
- **Identify potential pre-transition tax planning alternatives,**
- **Understand various strategies that are available for reducing tax when you sell your business, and**
- **Be aware of what choices you have for post-transition tax strategies.**

Taxation is a vast and complicated topic. For this reason, this chapter will only focus on issues that affect tax planning for your transition. We'll specifically look at strategies we have seen in use today that might help you reduce the income tax burden you could face in the three stages of transition: during pre-transition, when you are selling your business, and during post-transition. Nonetheless, tax planning shouldn't be limited to these stages of your life; some experts call it a "cradle to beyond the grave process," and we agree. The intent here is not to turn you into a tax guru. Rather, the purpose of this chapter is to give you a better understanding of the tax strategies available so that you can have greater input when working with the financial members of your transition advisory team. This is your future. Knowing what questions to ask can help you feel confident that you've left no "tax stone" unturned. Also, asking the right questions can often stimulate the creative planning process as it applies to your circumstances.

A Caveat before We Begin

Prior to implementing any tax strategy mentioned in this book, you should check with the appropriate members of your transition advisory team (accountant, financial planner/retirement planner) to make sure it is appropriate for your circumstances and it complies with the Income Tax Act (ITA), Canada Revenue Agency (CRA) requirements, interpretations, and practices. You might also want to make sure that your team members seek the counsel of an experienced tax specialist. Many advisors (including many accountants) are simply good tax generalists. In our experience, you don't need the expense of having a tax specialist on your team all of the time. It's enough that your other financial advisors know when to consult with one. Checking with such professionals will help to ensure that important details and procedures aren't overlooked. Finally, due to the constraints of space, the material provided here is in summary form only.

Overcoming the Tax Intimidation Factor

Albert Einstein once said, "The hardest thing to understand in the world is the income tax." Many people feel the same way. Just take a look at Canada's Income Tax Act. On one hand, it's contained in a book the size of a very large novel or biography. On the other hand, the wording can be so difficult and vague that its published interpretations, precedents, and practices take up what amounts to a fair-sized library!

The good news is that you don't need to have an in-depth knowledge of taxation to come out ahead at tax time. You simply need a qualified team of advisors, who can explain your options well enough to allow you to assess the advice and act on it. If your taxes are planned properly, there are literally tens of thousands and even hundreds of thousands of dollars that can be saved over a lifetime. As mentioned above, you might want to ask for a second opinion from a tax specialist if you think your situation, because of its complexity or the amount of money in question, warrants it.

McNulty's Coaching Advice

When it comes to tax planning, encourage your transition advisory team to be proactive and creative, while maintaining compliance with applicable laws and regulations at all times. Your ability to save tax isn't limited to the alternatives discussed in this book. Good tax planning should complement your present financial circumstances and enhance the likelihood of accomplishing your long-range financial goals.

General Categories for Reducing Income Tax Liability

Strategies to reduce income tax liability generally fall into the following three broad categories:

1. Income splitting

Canadians are subject to a marginal tax rate system, which means that as your income increases, so does the tax bite on those incremental dollars. Many thousands of dollars can be saved in tax every year by splitting income that would normally be taxed at the top marginal tax rate with someone in your family who is in a lower tax bracket. If it can be planned, for example, that a husband and wife residing in Newfoundland each earn $50,000 per year as opposed to one of them earning $100,000, the tax savings would be well over $8,000 per year in 2005. That's about a 10% raise in your disposable Cash Flow without having to work one more hour.

2. Tax deferral

Under the Canadian tax system, deferring tax can also make a great deal of sense. It's another category of commonly employed strategies. Your RRSP is a good example. Tax is deferred on deposits within prescribed limits to your RRSP, and on the money earned in your RRSP, until you take it out or until both you and your spouse have passed away. Incorporation is another method of tax deferral. The trick to getting the maximum benefit out of a tax deferral strategy is not just the initial deferral. It's also about bringing that deferred income back into your hands or the hands of another family member at a lower tax rate than that at which you deferred it. While it can take some planning, such strategies can often turn a deferral into actual savings. This is one reason why it's important to incorporate all three transition phases into one cohesive strategy. During the pre-transition and transition phases, you are basically laying the groundwork for turning tax deferrals into tax savings in the post-transition phase.

3. Income planning

Dividends and capital gains have a lower effective tax rate than earned income (salary, bonus, or the net from a proprietorship or your share of partnership profits) or interest income. For example, there can be a benefit in planning the optimum salary/dividend mix if you're professionally incorporated.

Using your RRSPs to hold interest-bearing assets is another example of income planning. By simply allocating these assets to a no-tax environment, such as an RRSP or IPP (individual pension plan), you'll benefit from higher annual compounding. Capital gains or dividends from Canadian companies are taxed at more favourable rates than interest income. If you earn such tax-favoured income in your RRSP, however, that advantageous tax treatment will be lost to you.

McNulty's Coaching Advice

If married, approach tax planning with an emphasis on your "average family" tax rate. Concentrating on strategies that reduce the taxes the whole family pays helps ensure that you're not leaving any stone unturned. To calculate your average family tax rate, take last year's tax returns from each family member and total up all the income. Now total up all the tax that was due on this income. Divide the tax paid by your total family income figure. The answer is your average family tax rate for the period.

Pre-Transition Tax Planning

This section discusses useful strategies for the period leading up to your transition that can lower your tax bite, facilitate your savings plan, and even contribute to reducing or eliminating your Resource Gap, if you have one.

Incorporation Can Offer a Combination of Benefits

This is an important pre-transition tax-planning strategy. Incorporation can combine the benefits of income splitting, tax deferral, and income planning.

Income splitting can be accomplished through the issue of dividends if your spouse and/or other family members (usually through a trust if they are not active in the business) own shares.

Tax deferral is possible in situations where your company is a Canadian-controlled private corporation (CCPC) that qualifies for the low combined federal and provincial tax rate on net active business income (not income from passive investments) below $300,000. For similar amounts of income earned in a proprietorship, a significant portion might be subject to the top marginal tax rate for individuals. This rate, as it applies to a CCPC on income under net $300,000, is lower than the normal corporate tax rate and significantly less than the highest personal marginal tax rate. In this situation, a deferral can result where such after-tax income is retained by the company as opposed to paying it all out to you in the form of salary or dividends.

Income planning relates to determining the optimum salary/dividend mix in your circumstances.

Business Debt Repayment

One excellent use of funds subject to the small-business tax rate, which are left in a corporation as compared to a proprietorship or partnership, is in the repayment of principal on business-related loans. While the interest on such debt would normally be deductible, paying back the principal is not. This means, if you operate as a proprietor or in a partnership, that repayment would have to come out of after-tax dollars. For example, if you're in a 46% tax bracket, to repay $100,000 of principal on a loan, you would have to earn, pre-tax in an unincorporated business, approximately $185,000. When the corporation pays principal back, it will have more money to do so. In a corporation with income under the small-business deduction threshold, assume the tax rate for such profits is 20%. To repay that same $100,000 from a corporation means the company would only have to earn $125,000 in after-tax profits. That's a big difference!

Other Expenses

While you do get a deduction when buying equipment or leaseholds in the way of the capital cost allowance, this benefit can typically only be fully realized over a long period of time. In the meantime, if you operate as a proprietor or in a partnership, you have had to either advance funds for the purchase out of after-tax income or borrow, the repayment of which would come out of after-tax income. Once again, if it's done through a corporation, there's a lot more money available after tax to make the purchase. Similarly, it can make a great deal of sense to have your corporation pay for non-deductible expenses that won't result in a taxable benefit to you—examples are life insurance and conventions in excess of two per year.

If you're a proprietor and have a negative proprietor's account (your balance sheet in your financial statements reflects liabilities that are greater than business assets), there can potentially be additional complications to consider if you are thinking about incorporating. These complications should be discussed with the appropriate financial members of your team.

This book deals with transition planning where there is a mature business that has already earned value. If you're dealing with a new business or one with little or no value, you might wish to talk to the appropriate advisor on your team about having your spouse and/or other family members subscribe for shares to facilitate income splitting in the future.

If you already have a corporation that has value where your spouse and/or other family members don't already own shares, you should be aware that there are additional complications to consider if you wish them to take ownership of a percentage of the firm. For example, if your spouse (who, under the ITA, doesn't deal with you at arm's length) were to purchase shares of the company, the price must be reflective of their fair market value (FMV). In a closely held corporation this could be somewhat difficult to establish. It's very important for the success of the long-term strategy that you are in a position to justify the price paid as being FMV if you're ever audited.

The following are a few possible ways for a non-arm's-length party to acquire shares of your mature company:

1. You could sell them some of your shares for their FMV. This could mean, depending on what your adjusted cost base (ACB) is for the shares, that you'll have to report a taxable capital gain on the sale. A capital gains exemption still exists for qualifying Canadian corporations, however, and you can't use it to shelter a non-arm's-length sale such as this.

2. You could have the non-arm's-length person subscribe for treasury shares, depending on how the share structure of your company is organized. Once again, the problem is that the price has to be FMV. This could

mean, for example, that your spouse has to borrow a significant amount of money to complete the purchase.

3. You could talk to your professional advisors to determine if a reorganization of your corporate share structure, referred to as a "freeze," might make sense. Briefly, this means that the value of the company at a particular point in time is "frozen." Preferred shares are issued to you to represent the frozen value of the company at that point. New common shares of nominal value are then issued to a combination of you and other family members, depending on your circumstances and exactly what you are trying to accomplish. The effect can be the sharing or even passing on of future growth to other family members and improved income-splitting flexibility. This process is very complex, so you would want to consult a tax specialist about it.

Professional Corporations

Professional corporations can be different from other types of companies, depending on the province where you reside. Some provinces limit ownership of the shares of a professional corporation to a member of the profession. This inhibits income splitting as compared to a normal company. If you reside in such a province, you might want to talk to your tax advisors about two corporations. One would be a professional corporation where you own the shares and the other an ordinary company that handles the non-professional components of your practice. The non-professional company would ideally be owned by your spouse or perhaps a trust where your spouse and children are the beneficiaries (see discussion below about association rules). If you've been supporting a relative such as an elderly parent, think about making them a beneficiary of the trust that owns shares in your corporation as well. Another difference is that the corporate structure does not shelter the owner from professional liability.

Professional incorporation is not for everyone. There can be a number of drawbacks to watch for. When it's first set up, you'll find it quite different from operating an unincorporated practice. For accountants and other financial advisors, working with companies like this is quite simple so they might not think it's necessary to provide you with any extra explanation or support. If you and your staff have been working in an unincorporated practice for your whole professional career, however, the change to a corporate structure can be confusing.

McNulty's Coaching Advice
Have your accountant or bookkeeper explain the differences between an unincorporated and an incorporated practice and walk you and your staff through what changes will have to be addressed and how to do so.

Setup costs can also be expensive and there are additional accounting and filing fees that you'll have to take into account. There is typically no protection from professional liability.

Partial Incorporation
Typically, this is a format used in professions subject to restrictive provincial incorporation rules of one kind or another. In such a situation, the non-professional aspects of their professional practices are sold or transferred to a corporation generally owned by their spouse and perhaps a trust for other family members. Such an action can offer greater income-splitting potential versus paying your spouse an appropriate salary. If your children are benefici-

aries of the trust and are over eighteen (see comments below on the "kiddie tax"), this structure would also facilitate greater income splitting with them.

Should You Have More than One Corporation?

Canadian-controlled private corporations (CCPCs), as mentioned earlier, are subject to a lower combined federal and provincial tax rate on active business profits under $300,000 per year. If your company has significant net active business earnings in excess of this small business limit, it would be great if you could just duplicate the benefit by setting up another CCPC. You won't be surprised to hear that it's not all that simple. If it was, everyone would keep setting up more companies as they hit the $300,000 threshold in the one(s) they already had. This would defeat the intention of the small business deduction. To prevent this from happening, the Income Tax Act contains what are known as "association rules." They are very complex. These rules effectively require that the small business limit be shared among companies deemed to be associated.

It's possible for people who don't deal at arms-length to own companies that are associated. We know of a case where a husband owns the shares of a car rental agency. His spouse owns 100% of the shares of a company that operates a car wash close by. There's no cross ownership of shares. Both companies enjoy their own small-business tax rate on active profits. Talk to your advisors to see if there's any possibility this would make sense in your circumstances.

Consider a Management Company

If you own a corporation or a proprietorship with a significant amount of general and administrative expenses, you might want to discuss the concept of a hiring a management company owned by your spouse and perhaps a trust for your children who are over eighteen to provide management services to your enterprise. Let's say you're the sole shareholder of a company that has about $1,000,000 in expenses. If you contracted with the management company to provide management services to your corporation that included paying all of these expenses on its behalf, the charges for this service could be up to 15% of such expenses. That's $150,000 of income. Now, the company will have expenses but at the end of the day, it could mean that significantly more income was channelled into the hands of other family members than would have been possible by the payment of a salary that's in compliance with CRA guidelines. Your advisors might also be able to structure the arrangement so that this income is subject to the small-business tax rate if your children are over the age of eighteen or if your spouse is the sole shareholder. GST is payable on management fees, so this wouldn't work if you are in a profession that is zero-rated or tax-exempt because you couldn't claim input tax credits.

Additional Pre-Transition Income Splitting Alternatives

Many retirement planners recommend that the RRSPs of both spouses should be roughly equal in order to facilitate income splitting upon retirement. This rule of thumb needs additional definition for a business owner. In many businesses or professions, the owner has a much higher income than the spouse, which can result in a disproportionate buildup of investment assets in the business owner's name. If most of the family's investments are in the business owner's name, the resulting investment income could all be subject to the top marginal tax rate. Therefore, the strategy wouldn't be to simply equalize RRSPs but rather investments in general.

McNulty's Coaching Advice

To equalize your holdings between each spouse, you might want to consider having your spouse save his or her salary for investment purposes and using your income to pay for living expenses. If your spouse saves his or her income for the family's financial security, you should separate funds allocated out of your income for that spouse's personal spending money and other needs. It can be very demeaning for a spouse to ask for money. In our experience, financial strategies of this nature work more effectively if both spouses have personal funds they can spend as they see fit.

Splitting Earned Income

Employing a spouse or a child (who is legally old enough to work) is one of the most common methods used by independent business people for income splitting. When it comes to earned income (from the business salary, for example), Canada Revenue Agency (CRA) takes the position that you should pay someone who's related to you the same as you would pay someone who's not related to you for the same work. Many business owners pay their spouses a significant earned income. The justification for this from CRA's perspective is that the spouse performs some form of important role in the firm. The greater the responsibility, the larger the salary generally paid in the open market. Rather than describing your spouse as a bookkeeper or something similar, you might want to rearrange his or her duties to justify a more important position such as vice-president of finance. Whether you pay your spouse an executive income or not, they should have a job description on file. Before putting the description in place, check the wording with your legal and tax transition advisory team members.

Another benefit of splitting earned income with a spouse is that he or she will be able to make RRSP contributions. If you're unsure whether your spouse's compensation package would be considered reasonable, discuss it with the financial members of your advisory team. They can't give you any absolutes or guarantees but they should have the experience to tell you what's reasonable and what's not. You might also want to check with your professional advisors to consider strategies such as employee profit-sharing plans in order to avoid CPP contributions and the cost of EI in some circumstances.

Attribution Rules

Attribution rules prevent you from shifting investment income (dividends and interest) to a spouse or minor child who's in a lower income tax bracket. Under these rules, if you were to loan money at no interest or gift money to your spouse for investment purposes, the resulting dividends or interest would be "attributed" back to you for tax purposes, thus defeating the strategy. This has resulted in a significant amount of time and creative energy going into designing ways of splitting investment income that won't be caught in the "attribution net." Briefly, some of these alternatives are:

1. Trusts and the kiddie tax

After-tax corporate profits are commonly distributed by providing dividends to shareholders. In the past, you could split income with your kids, regardless of age, by having a trust for the benefit of your children own shares of your company and paying them dividends through that trust. It worked really well! Depending on the amount paid out, these dividends might not have attracted any tax at all. However, the rules changed a few years ago. Now if dividends are paid in this manner, where the beneficiary is under the age of eighteen, they'll attract tax at the highest rate. It's therefore no longer prudent to split income this way. Once a child turns eighteen, however, this strategy starts to be effective again. If you have a trust where the beneficiaries are minors, talk to the appropriate advisor on your team to determine if it would make sense to have a holding company between your operating company and the trust. Dividends could then be collected in the holding company but not paid out to the trust until a child reaches the age of majority.

2. Capital gains trusts

There's no attribution of capital gains for funds loaned to a trust for a minor child or children (not spouses). A trust used in this manner is sometimes referred to as a capital gains trust. The caution here is that most investments that earn capital gains also earn dividends, and only capital gains are exempt from the attribution rules. If the trust earns dividend income by investing the funds you've loaned to it, that income will be attributed back to you for tax purposes. But when that income is attributed to you, as the higher income member of the family, you shouldn't pay any more tax than you would have paid if the dividends came directly into your hands. Another important thing to keep in mind is that capital losses are also not attributed.

3. Investment portfolio

If your investment portfolio is significantly higher than your spouse's and you need to equalize, one alternative to investigate is the purchase of an asset from him or her for its fair market value. When the spouse invests the proceeds, there should be no concern about attribution of the income.

Case Study

In reviewing the financial circumstances of a new client, we noticed that his non-registered investment portfolio, which was in excess of $1,000,000, was producing significant investment income. His wife, on the other hand, didn't have much earned income and had almost no investments. They jointly owned a house, free and clear of any liabilities, valued at $750,000. By having the client purchase the spouse's share of the house for $375,000, it was possible to invest the money in her name without attribution. This resulted in significant tax savings that year and a reduction in the family's average tax rate. It also helped with long-term post-transition tax planning.

4. Secondary income (for those with a non-registered investment portfolio)

This concept is best explained with an example. Suppose you have an investment portfolio of $500,000 of unregistered assets earning a return of 5%. Of course, any income that it earns will be taxed in your hands. Now let's say you have a trust in place for your minor children who are well under the age of eighteen. You could loan that $500,000 to the trust. When the trust earned the return of 5%, it would be attributed back to you for tax purposes. This doesn't mean you received it. The money is still in the trust. You just have to pay tax on it.

These earnings are now the property of the trust. If invested for five years, the trust could have say $ 138,140 capital of its own accumulated. At 5%, this means the following year almost $7,000 would be taxed in the hands of your children rather than your hands. In other words, it wouldn't be subject to your high rate of tax. Depending on your circumstances and the age of your children, the resulting tax savings could grow dramatically over the years. Keep in mind that to accomplish this strategy, you should not have to pay any more tax than if you had not taken steps to implement the strategy. By the way, the original capital would be loaned on a demand note basis so that as the trustee you could simply require the trust to pay it back whenever you wished.

5. Spousal RRSPs

You make the contribution, get the tax deduction, but the asset builds in your spouse's name for use in retirement. What could be easier? Spousal RRSPs are great for setting up income-splitting arrangements in retirement.

6. Registered Education Savings Plans (RESP)

While not contributing directly to your transition plan, RESPs are a good way of splitting income and saving for your children's education, thereby freeing up other resources that can be devoted to your transition plan. There's also the Canada Education Savings Grant, which is 20% of the contribution to a maximum of $400 per annum per child (there is a cumulative maximum per child of $7,200).

Tax Deferral: Pre-Transition

RRSPs are generally the most commonly used vehicle for tax deferral. The deferral comes when the initial deposit is made because it's deductible (provided you don't over-contribute) from your taxable income. Deferral also results when the income within the RRSP trust compounds on a tax-free basis. It's important to keep in mind that the maximum benefit comes from making deposits that are deductible at the top marginal rate.

Remember that tax must be paid when funds are eventually withdrawn from the RRSP. Therefore, if your spouse is in a low tax bracket, you might want to consider whether or not it makes sense to make his or her contribution at a particular point in time. It might be better to have the low-income spouse accumulate funds outside of the RRSP, even though it could result in some current tax at a low marginal rate. The RRSP carry-forward rules allow you to accumulate the ability to make a contribution. In the meantime, you could consider strategies to increase the spouse's income up to the point that a deposit to an RRSP would result in a significant deferral.

There's another planning twist that can make good sense in the right circumstances. A low-income spouse can make the RRSP contribution but choose not to take the deduction in that year. This way, the investment grows tax-free and you can consider strategies to increase taxable income in the future to the point where the deduction can be taken in a year when a significant deferral results.

Retirement Compensation Arrangements (RCA)

Retirement Compensation Arrangements can offer significant income-splitting and tax-deferral benefits for the unincorporated proprietorship that employs a spouse or for the business owner and his or her spouse if they're employees of a corporation that one or both of them own. Generally, the greatest advantage is realized from this supplemental retirement planning tool if it's set up at a time when you or your spouse are over age fifty, have earned a significant income from the business or salary from the corporation subject to the top marginal rate, and don't have too much accumulated in RRSPs. But we're getting ahead of ourselves.

First let's define an RCA. It's an arrangement whereby an employer makes a tax-deductible contribution to a custodian for the benefit of an employee (you or your spouse). If you're incorporated, the company would be the employer and you and perhaps your spouse would be the employee. The custodian sends 50% of the contribution to the Canada Revenue Agency (CRA) where the money is set aside in a *refundable* tax account. The other 50% is deposited into an RCA trust for the benefit of the employee (you or your spouse). The money in the trust is then invested.

There are really no rules when it comes to what the trust can invest in, unlike, for example, an RRSP. When the trust earns money on the assets invested within it, 50% of those earnings also go to CRA where they get added to your RCA refundable tax account. When the employee (you or your spouse) retires and starts to draw income from the RCA trust, CRA will send $1 back from the refundable tax account to the trust for every $2 the trust pays out. Sound confusing?

Let's look at a quick example. Suppose the RCA paid out $20,000 during the year. CRA would send $10,000 from the refundable tax account back to the RCA. The net effect would be that the funds in the RCA trust went down by $10,000 and the funds in the refundable tax account went down by $10,000. When the trust pays out income to the beneficiary, it's taxable. So if you're required to send money to CRA for the refundable tax account and then must pay tax when the money is paid out, where's the advantage, you might ask.

Basically, the funds you deposit with the custodian for the RCA should all be deductible at the top marginal rate of tax. When that money is brought back into income, provided proper planning has taken place, it should be subject to a much lower tax rate which results in a net savings.

In the right circumstances, this can be a very powerful planning tool. Fundamentally, you would be making the contributions with funds that would have been, for the most part, going to pay tax anyway, with no chance of that money ever being returned.

Another advantage is that it can be used as a tool to equalize retirement assets between spouses so that the post-transition average family tax rate is kept to a minimum. It can also offer some strategic benefits to those who are doing a full transition early in life, say in their mid to late fifties or even early sixties. In the past, we've been able to effectively use income from an RCA to fund living needs without having to draw on RRSPs prior to the beneficiary's reaching age sixty-nine. That leaves the money in the RRSP to compound for a longer period of time. RCAs can also be useful in planning around the time you sell your business.

Tax-Deferral Benefits of Incorporation

Incorporation offers great deferral benefits if the funds aren't needed for your immediate Cash Flow and can be left in the company, as mentioned earlier.

Individual Pension Plans (IPP)

An IPP is a registered pension plan that is set up via the corporation for you and/or your spouse (if he or she works for your company). Contribution limits can be significantly higher for an IPP than the maximum RRSP deduction limit. This means a greater deduction and more assets growing tax-free for your retirement. IPPs also offer the added benefit of being protected from creditors.

If you (and/or your spouse) have worked in your corporation as an employee for many years without a pension plan in place, talk to the appropriate advisor on your transition team about an IPP and what's known as a *past-service contribution*. Past-service contributions can result in significant tax deductions over and above normal contribution levels. A credible actuary should be able to provide you with the answers you need regarding the details of the potential past-service contribution and how to go about doing it.

McNulty's Coaching Advice

When it comes time for your transition, it's possible that additional funds could be set aside on a deductible basis in an Individual Pension Plan (IPP) that would allow you to retire early and have greater spousal benefits or indexing. This is only possible if you've been an employee of a corporation for a number of years. While they offer many advantages, IPPs aren't for everyone. An IPP can be costly to set up and maintain. Also, it can be complex to administer. Careful analysis should be done to ensure that an IPP is right for you before proceeding. A combination of RRSPs and RCAs might be a better alternative.

Universal Life Insurance As a Tax Strategy

Universal life as an insurance alternative is discussed under Risk Management in chapter ten. It combines permanent life insurance with the possibility of tax-free growth for the cash that's intended to build up in the policy, within prescribed limits. This cash that builds up in the policy is often referred to as cash surrender value (CSV). When promoted as a retirement planning alternative, the strategy usually involves the policy in combination with a loan from a financial institution.

If you have CSV built up in a universal life policy and then upon retirement decide to have some of this CSV paid out to support your retirement living needs, the withdrawals would attract some tax. Life insurance is only tax-free when the benefit is paid out upon the death of the insured. The purpose of the loan is to avoid such tax while you're alive. There's no income tax on borrowed funds. Similarly, there are strategies whereby such universal life policies are owned by your corporation. These strategies are sometimes called insured retirement plans, and at first glance, the concept seems to make a lot of sense.

If structured properly, the savings component of a universal life policy grows tax-free. When you want to use it to help fund your retirement, rather than taking out the CSV and paying the resulting tax, you borrow (within limits) from a financial institution that takes the policy as security. On the death of the insured, proceeds from the life insurance are tax-free. They're first used to pay off the financial institution and the balance goes to your beneficiaries or estate.

Sounds pretty good, doesn't it? Like so many things, however, on closer inspection there are some concerns. For example, in many of the proposals we've seen, the assumptions employed are questionable. There are also expensive costs to be factored in and your money has to be tied up for a long period of time. We therefore strongly recommend that an advisor who isn't connected with the sale of the policy carefully analyze any such offerings. The advisor should also have an excellent understanding of your overall needs, what other alternatives are available, and the nuances of such insurance product offerings. Ask them to check into the new policies that are now available from some insurance companies that have significantly reduced front-end loading.

Tax Shelters

Tax shelters can be very complex investments. They typically offer investors either tax deferral or a combination of tax deferral and actual tax savings. In our experience, they're great tax shelters because they lose so much money!

Often the promotional material with these kinds of investments mentions that an advance tax ruling has been obtained from Canada Revenue Agency. It's important that you understand that these rulings can still leave the investment open to attack from CRA. The advance rulings don't express an opinion on whether or not the business that's the subject of the tax shelter has a reasonable expectation of profit, which is a reason why many of these shelters get reassessed. If the main benefit of the proposed venture is tax savings as opposed to income (not capital gains), be very cautious. We strongly recommend that you get an opinion from a knowledgeable member of your transition team. Make sure it's not someone involved in any way with the sale or distribution of the tax shelter.

Pre-Transition Income Planning

Canada Pension Plan (CPP)

The maximum required CPP contribution in 2005 is a little more than $3,700. Contributions are supposed to be made between the ages of eighteen and seventy if you are receiving a salary. Depending on your age, if you've been making contributions at the maximum level for many years there's a possibility that you already qualify for the maximum benefit available under this government pension scheme or very close to the maximum. If you think this could be the case, you can obtain a statement from CRA that tells you what your benefit would be right now. Perhaps you are one of those people who feel they will never actually receive this government pension, either because of the strain the baby boomers will put on it or because of the passing into law of a "means test." That is, regulations that could be put in place stating that if your income or assets are over a defined threshold, the CPP benefit could be clawed back. Or you might simply be financially independent and not willing to pay into a government pension program that you have no control over.

If any of the above accurately describes your situation, you might want to talk to your professional advisors about an employee profit sharing plan (EPSP). Income that's reasonable within the circumstances and paid through such a plan is deductible to your corporation the same way that salary is deducted. It also qualifies as earned income for the purpose of calculating your RRSP or pension contribution limit. Having an EPSP can eliminate the need for you to make these expensive CPP contributions. In our experience, EPSPs are not expensive to set up and are reasonably easy to administrate.

The Salary/Dividend Mix

Dividends paid from a Canadian corporation entitle the recipient to a tax credit to allow for the fact that the corporation has already paid some tax on that money. Issuing a combination of dividends and salary might result in some tax savings over a salary alone. Keep in mind, though, that dividends don't qualify as "earned income." They're paid out of after-tax corporate earnings. Salary or bonuses paid to you are earned income and paid before tax from the company.

You must have some earned income to continue to make RRSP, IPP, or even RCA contributions. If you have a corporation, talk to your professional advisor about planning the optimum salary/dividend mix for your circumstances. If you're close to transition and financially independent, ask your professional advisor to review the pros and cons of making another RRSP contribution versus paying out money in dividends and building a "tax paid" pool of capital.

Income planning also applies to your investments. Remember that it's prudent to arrange to have your interest-bearing assets grow in a tax-free or low-tax environment such as an RRSP or properly constructed universal life policy. Assets that earn dividends and capital gains that receive favourable tax treatment should ideally be held outside of "no tax" or "low tax" environments.

McNulty's Coaching Advice

In the pre-transition planning phase of your life, build up a non-registered investment portfolio that isn't in a corporation. In other words, this portfolio would be a pool of tax-paid capital. Once you fully retire, the use of non-registered capital will be important to keep your average family tax rate at a minimum level.

Strategies for Reducing Tax When You Sell Your Business

You have a number of alternative strategies to consider for reducing the tax impact on the sale of your business. In tax planning, a great deal depends on your particular circumstances. Are you incorporated? Does your spouse work for the business? Is he or she a shareholder? Are you a member of a partnership? Do you have sizable tax-shelter losses? What about any capital losses? Depending on how you answered those questions, some of the following might be suitable for you:

1. The structure of many purchase agreements makes allowances for the spouse of the vendor to provide some consulting to the purchaser for a fee. The consulting fee should qualify as earned income for your spouse. This could mean that he or she will have a higher RRSP contribution limit the following year.

2. No matter whether you are a proprietor, in a partnership, or the owner of a corporation, if your spouse has worked for you for a fair length of time (prior to 1996), you could pay him or her a retiring allowance within prescribed limits that can be rolled into his or her RRSP without immediate tax. Similarly, if your business is incorporated and you yourself have been an employee since prior to 1996, the corporation might be able to pay you a deductible retiring allowance that can be rolled into your RRSP. An employer can make a tax-deductible payment to a retiring employee in the form of a retiring allowance. The interesting thing about a retiring allowance is that, within limits, it can be "rolled" directly into the employee's RRSP without any withholding tax under special rules relating to such pay-

ments. The formula works this way: for years of service prior to 1989, the employee can roll $3,500 per year into his or her RRSP, provided he or she was not a member of a vested pension plan. For years of service from 1989 to 1995, $2,000 per year of service can be "rolled" tax-free into the employee's RRSP. That's seven years. So if you and your spouse have worked for your corporation since 1970, you could pay a retiring allowance to each of you when the business is sold that is deductible to the company and that can be rolled tax-free into your respective RRSPs of $77,000 [(18 years x $3,500) + (7 years x $2,000)] each.

3. You could make a Retirement Compensation Arrangement (RCA) contribution for your spouse's benefit, if he or she has worked for your proprietorship or corporation for a sufficient length of time. If you own an incorporated business where you've been an employee, it's also possible that the company could make an RCA contribution to a plan for you. The only guidelines in the Income Tax Act about how much can be put into an RCA are that the contributions must be reasonable within the circumstances. Our experience with CRA is that they'll consider a contribution "reasonable within the circumstances" if it's based on a formula relating to the employee's years of service, income, and present RRSP or IPP level. Due to the complexity of the funding formula, have the financial members of your transition advisory team do the calculation, or hire an actuary.

4. You may be able to sell shares of your corporation and claim the capital gains exemption. Qualifying shares of Canadian-controlled private corporations (CCPC) are eligible for a capital gains exemption. It's often referred to as the *super exemption*. This is part of the lifetime capital gains exemption (CGE) of $500,000. If you used the $100,000 CGE when it was available to individuals, then you would only have $400,000 left. Incidentally, if your spouse and/or

other family members own shares of your CCPC, then it's also possible that they would be able to claim this CGE on a share sale.

There are some rules about how a company's shares qualify for this super exemption that you should discuss with the appropriate advisors on your team. For example, at least 50% of the company's assets must have been invested in the production of active business income for two years prior to the sale. Further, at the time of the sale, a minimum of 90% of the company's assets must be invested in the production of active business income.

While selling shares and sheltering the tax with the CGE might seem like an excellent way to sell your business and save a lot of tax, it's not that simple. While it's great for the vendor, it's not necessarily good for the purchaser. There are no tax deductions by way of depreciation for buying shares. For this reason, the purchaser would often rather buy the assets of the business. In this way, they could benefit from the capital cost allowance (depreciation) available on the various asset classes. So what's the moral of the story? If you're incorporated and want to sell the shares to utilize the capital gains exemption, you can expect any interested buyers to negotiate to share some of the benefits. Selling shares versus assets will even change the way the valuation is conducted.

McNulty's Coaching Advice

If you're working with a credible valuator, ask them what price the shares of your corporation might command in the market place versus a more traditional asset sale. Then ask your professional advisors to analyze the pros and cons of this strategy versus the combination of an asset sale and other strategies mentioned here. And most important, before deciding on this strategy, talk to your professional advisors to make sure you don't have

Cumulative Net Investment Losses (CNIL). Things like tax-shelter deductions, rental losses, and carrying charges create a CNIL balance. A CNIL balance reduces or eliminates your ability to claim the capital gains exemption (CGE).

5. You could sell the company's assets rather than the company. From the purchaser's point of view, there's no difference between selling assets and buying an unincorporated proprietorship. The benefit for you, the vendor, is the corporation's low rate of tax below the small-business deduction levels (as mentioned earlier). In this case, you would enjoy a deferral of the tax until such time as the money is paid out of the company. For the portion of the goodwill that would represent the other 50% that isn't taxable, the money could be paid as a dividend to you absolutely tax-free. This is due to some special rules relating to what's called a capital dividend account. The balance of the money in the corporation could then be paid out over a period of years. If the sale would create a significant amount of income over the small-business deduction threshold, strategies such as a retiring allowance or RCA could be useful in reducing profits to the required level.

6. The timing of the sale of your business could save you tax, whether you're incorporated or not. If you're not incorporated, do not plan to work much once the business is sold and have a calendar year-end—the best day to set as a closing date for the sale would be January 1st. Everyone's personal year-end for tax purposes is December 31st. Selling as of January 1st could mean a large portion of the resulting income would be taxed at a rate that would benefit from the lower marginal tax rate levels and your personal tax credit. Let us explain further with an example.

Case Study

"Sam" received an offer of $592,500 for the purchase of his unincorporated business. Based on the allocation of various asset classes (goodwill, leaseholds, equipment, etc.), taxable income from the sale was estimated to be $320,000. The terms of sale did not require Sam to stay on in the business for any length of time. In this case, he could leave whenever he wanted. Sam's fiscal year-end is the calendar year. During the year (2001), it was estimated that the business would earn a net of $265,000. Sam is a resident of Manitoba where the top marginal tax rate is 43.7%. If the sale were to close in December of 2001, the total amount of taxable income the sale would generate would be taxed at 43.7% (the top rate at the time). This would mean that the tax on the sale without any planning would be $139,840. On the other hand, if the closing had been arranged for January 1, 2002, and it could also be arranged that Sam would have no other taxable income in 2002, then the tax payable would be over $10,000 less. That's not a bad savings for a one-day change!

7. Accruing a bonus to an employee that's deductible from the corporation's income is another strategy that relates to timing, if you're incorporated. In this case, you would need a year-end less than six months before December 31st. It's possible for a corporation to accrue a bonus to an employee (you and perhaps your spouse) that's deductible from the corporation's income but not taxable to the employee until it's paid out. This applies as long as it's paid within 179 days of the year-end. Assume you sold all the assets of your company (not the shares) in March of a particular year. Also assume that you wouldn't work more than the time required to facilitate the transfer of goodwill to the new owners, perhaps a period of no more than eight months. As of your year-end, July 31st, if net income is in excess of the $300,000 small business threshold, you might

want to declare a bonus to you as a strategy to reduce your corporate tax exposure. If paying that bonus right away would mean all or most of it would get taxed at the top marginal rate, by having your corporate year-end at the end of July you could defer payment of that bonus into the next taxation year. At that point it might be possible, depending on how you structure your income, to pay a lot less tax on it; you would benefit from the use of your personal tax credit and the marginal tax rate system would start to work for you.

Alternatively, if you're incorporated but in a business or profession where for one reason or another you can't sell it for a material sum, you might want to discuss reducing the payment of your salary for that final year before retirement. This strategy would only apply if your income expectation in the corporation, by not taking a salary, would remain below the $300,000 small-business taxation threshold. The amount you defer should be any income that would be taxed at the top marginal tax rates that you can afford to leave in the corporation. The benefit would be an additional deferral. To consider this strategy, you would either not need the money to pay your lifestyle expenses, or you would have the available tax-paid funds to supplement your living needs for the balance of the year.

Section Three:
Post-Transition Tax Strategies

A great deal has been written about RRSP maturity options, CPP, old age security, and other forms of retirement income. In the interest of brevity, we won't comment in detail on the mechanics of these sources of retirement funding. It's already been covered elsewhere. Instead, this segment will focus on their implications for tax planning.

McNulty's Coaching Advice

Good post-transition tax strategies are the result of sound planning and organization in the pre-transition phase of your life. Whenever considering strategies suggested to you, ask about both the immediate impact and about how it will affect your tax position once you've retired. The best strategies have a long-term beneficial impact!

Old Age Security (OAS)

One factor that can influence your post transition planning is Old Age Security. OAS is an indexed government program that provides income to all Canadians aged sixty-five or older. In 2005, the estimated benefit, which is paid monthly, should amount to over $5,700 per spouse annually. That's in excess of $11,400 annually for two qualifying spouses. Over your retirement life, OAS benefits could add up to hundreds of thousands of dollars.

While OAS is potentially a great benefit, there is a proverbial fly in the ointment. In this case, it's a graduated claw-back of OAS benefits. An estimate for the start of the clawback threshold for 2006 is when the individual's taxable income exceeds $60,806. The benefit is completely clawed back when taxable income reaches $98,700. The

OAS claw-back is based on your taxable income in the previous year. Should you be subject to this claw-back, it will be held back from ongoing payments as opposed to you having to write a cheque at the end of the year when you file your tax return.

Many retirement strategies are intended to help you save tax and also leave you in a position to benefit from this government program. It is therefore important to plan your post-transition strategies so that you can take advantage of the OAS payments, if not forever, then at least for as long as possible. By using a combination of capital encroachment from sources of tax-paid capital and income from investments, RRSPs or pensions, corporate dividends, and so on, it's possible for many retired business owners to keep their taxable income below the claw-back level mentioned above. This means that not only can you enjoy the OAS income but your income taxes will also be at a lower level.

Tax Characteristics of Various Retirement Capital Pools

In your pre-transition planning, it's prudent to build capital with your post-transition needs in mind. These funds may be in RRSPs, IPPs, RCAs, corporations, insurance policies, and what can be thought of as open or non-registered investments. Think of each of these vehicles as "pools" of retirement capital. The tax characteristics of these pools of retirement capital are as follows:

1. *RRSPs must be converted to one of the approved alternatives in the year you turn age sixty-nine.* There are three broad categories of options to which you can convert your RRSP (assuming you aren't simply going to cash them in). The first is an annuity and the second is a Registered Retirement Income Fund (RRIF). Any income you receive from your RRSP directly or after you've converted it either

to a RRIF or annuity is 100% taxable. If you have an IPP or if your spouse has a pension plan entitlement, the resulting income will also be 100% taxable as well. The third option isn't very practical. You can collapse the plan and take the money out. Of course, that would mean the accumulated value would all represent taxable income that year, which could well mean a significant portion of your retirement savings will be paid in tax.

2. Payments out of an RCA and pension are 100% taxable.

3. Should you have funds built up in a corporation, when you take the money out it will be taxable as either dividends or perhaps a salary or a mix of the two, depending on your circumstances.

4. Government benefits such as OAS and CPP are taxable as regular income to you. The maximum CPP benefit for 2005 is almost $10,000 and like OAS, the benefits are indexed. It's common for spouses not to qualify for the maximum CPP benefit, and in cases such as these, it's possible to split your CPP benefit with your spouse. This can be a simple way to reduce your tax burden if your spouse is in a lower marginal income tax bracket than you.

5. Capital gains and dividends are effectively taxed more favourably than interest income. Only 50% of capital gains are taxable. Dividends benefit from the dividend tax credit, which is intended as a way of making up to the owner of the stock for the fact that the company has already paid tax on the corporate income at its rate.

6. Using non-registered capital to support your retirement daily living needs doesn't create any tax in and of itself. This makes non-registered capital an important planning tool.

7. The equity you have in personal-use assets such as your house or cottage can be strategically used in retirement to minimize tax. This equity isn't taxable, so if there's no other non-registered capital to encroach on, it might be possible to use some of these assets to supplement your Cash Flow. In this way, you won't have to take income from a taxable source any earlier than necessary that would put you into a much higher tax bracket or bring about a claw-back of your OAS benefits.

The assets could be used to access funds through an instrument such as a reverse mortgage or a home line of credit. We prefer these two alternatives to a traditional mortgage because the payments required by a normal amortization can impact your retirement Cash Flow. There's a way of using the equity you have in your personal-use assets with borrowed money, where the interest is deductible. First, sell the investment assets (assuming you're not going to be triggering any big capital gain). Then, put the money into the bank or a money market fund to supplement your retirement Cash Flow and borrow the funds to buy back the assets on the open market by using your personal-use asset as security. If you're thinking of doing this and claiming a capital loss on your tax return, discuss it with the appropriate advisor on your team.

It should be emphasized that borrowing should never be undertaken without a thorough analysis. Borrowing for investment purposes will increase your risk level. Before taking this step, review the strategy with your financial advisors. If you have an RCA, ask them about using the funds in the RCA trust to put a mortgage on your home or cottage as a way of using these funds in a tax-efficient manner. From an estate-planning perspective, if your health is good, you might want to consider buying a term-to-100 insurance policy (assuming you don't already have one) and assigning it to the bank. In that way, if something should happen to you, the loan would be paid off and the personal-use asset would be free and clear for your survivor or heir(s).

8. Borrowing against the CSV of your permanent life insurance contract can be a source of non-taxable cash. Once again, the insurance portion of the contract would be assigned to the bank to pay off the loan when you pass on.

McNulty's Coaching Advice

In late fall of each year, meet with your financial advisors to determine the following:
• what your income needs are likely to be over the coming calendar year
• what return expectations might be
• if there have been any changes that will impact your retirement strategies
• the optimum use of your asset pools for the coming year in terms of withdrawals

Planning your retirement income on an annual basis is an important activity. It's your job to tell your advisor how much money you think you'll need in order to finance your expenditures. It's their job to figure out if you can afford to spend this sum, given your financial resources, and to work out the best withdrawal mix from the various pools of capital that are available to you, from a tax perspective.

Specific Strategies for Post-Transition Tax Reduction

1. Once you reach age sixty-five, you're entitled to a pension income tax credit. If you don't have any pension income, take the $1,000 minimum required from both your and your spouse's RRSPs and offset the tax liability with this pension income tax credit.

2. If you have non-registered investments that are generating so much income that you'll exceed the threshold for the OAS clawback, ask your financial advisor to analyze the pros and cons of setting up a holding company into which you would transfer some or all of those income-producing assets. The transfer could be accomplished on a tax-free basis using an election in the Income Tax Act (ITA). The holding company is a separate taxpayer. It might help you to manage your income so that you avoid the claw-back.

3. If you're age sixty-five or older and your income is so high that the OAS benefits are being clawed back or if a significant portion of your assets have accrued gains on them, you might want to talk to your financial advisor about setting up an "Alter Ego Trust." This is a trust set up when you are alive to which you can transfer assets on a tax-deferred basis. Only you and your spouse should be entitled to receive any income or capital from the trust. This is a costly and complicated strategy and not for everyone. We recommend, once again, that you go over it with your professional advisor.

4. If you have interest-bearing investments outside of your registered plan and investments such as stocks that earn capital gains and/or dividend income within your RRSP, you might want to consider exchanging them. In this way, the interest income, rather than attracting tax as regular income, will instead benefit from the tax-free compounding available in the registered environment. Dividend income from Canadian corporations also qualifies for the dividend tax credit. When capital gains or dividends are earned in a registered environment, this tax advantage is lost. When possible, earn interest in the registered plans and dividends and capital gains outside such plans. Generally, you can make such changes either by selling your non-registered assets and using the cash to purchase the stocks or equity-based mutual funds from the registered plan for fair market value or you can do an exchange. If you elect to do an exchange, keep in mind that it must be at fair market value. There's one important point to keep in mind in this situation: you cannot deduct capital losses if the asset you're transferring to the registered plan is worth less than what you paid for it. Once again, check with your financial advisor to work out the mechanics.

5. RRSPs must be converted to a RRIF, LIF, or annuity by December 31st of the year that the annuitant turns sixty-nine. If you've earned income in the year you turn age sixty-nine, you might want to consider making an over-contribution to your RRSP in late December. RRSP contributions are based on 18% of the previous year's earned income. Since RRSP contributions can't be made after the year in which you turn sixty-nine, it's possible that you could lose the RRSP deduction capability for that year. Over-contributions to RRSPs are fined at the rate of 1% per month. The way the rules are currently written, by making an over-contribution in December, you would only have to pay the 1% penalty for one month. The following January, you would be back onside with the contribution rules.

6. If you've earned income and are over the age of sixty-nine, it's no longer possible to make contributions to your own RRSP, but it is possible to make contributions to a spousal plan for your spouse if they're under the age of seventy.

7. When you convert your RRSP to an RRIF, you don't have to start taking income right away. In fact, you can delay it until the next year. Thus, if you converted your RRSPs to an RRIF in September of 2004, you wouldn't have to take out any money until 2005. The longer you can leave that money in the registered plan, the greater the tax-free compounding benefit. Therefore, if you don't need the money to live on, arrange for the minimum RRIF payment to be made.

8. The formula for calculating the minimum RRIF payment is age-dependant. The younger you are, the less money has to be paid out. You do have the option to base the RRIF pay-out formula either on your age or that of your spouse. If your spouse is younger than you are, basing the formula on his or her age will mean that you have a lower minimum payout requirement. If you don't need the money to live on, this will reduce current taxes and leave more funds to compound tax-free for a longer period. Keep in mind that if you need more money in a given period, you can always increase the amount coming out of the RRIF.

9. A prescribed annuity can be an efficient way to earn tax-efficient income on interest-bearing investments. A prescribed annuity is not purchased with registered funds from an RRSP. In this case, you use non-registered funds. Prescribed annuities offer a significant advantage. There are two components to the money paid out under a pre-scribed annuity. One is non-taxable Cash Flow. The other is the tax component. The nice feature of a prescribed annuity is that the taxable portion is often quite low. It can amount to a significant deferral when compared to holding a portion of your portfolio in interest-bearing investments in order to supply your income needs and pay the tax accordingly.

10. If you change your Canadian residence, you might benefit from a lower or even a zero-tax regulatory environment. Canadians are taxed on residence, so if you're a Canadian resident, Canadian tax laws apply. If you live outside of Canada, payments from your registered plans or an RCA might only be subject to a Canadian withholding tax, depending on the tax treaty with the country in which you reside. These withholding taxes might be substantially lower than the tax you would be faced with as a Canadian resident. This is a very complex area and if you would like to explore it further, get a referral to a credible legal or accounting firm that specializes in this topic.

In summary, sound tax planning isn't always about one or two big actions that save buckets of tax. It often involves a number of little "bucket" strategies. Saving $5,000 here, $2,000 there, $7,000 elsewhere, and so on adds up to real money. This is particularly true, thankfully, when you consider the cumulative impact over a number of years.

Chapter Nine
Investment Strategies for Financial Independence and Transition

This chapter will help you:
- **Understand the twelve principles or investment rules we've found to be most successful for business owners,**
- **Understand what a formal investment strategy is and the benefits of using one, and**
- **Establish an investment strategy that complements your individual circumstances, constraints, and transition plans.**

Investment Philosophy: Converting Your Investment Portfolio into a Pension

An ideal final transition from your business means you have built up an investment portfolio that will support your ongoing lifestyle needs, post-transition. In other words, when you complete your transition, all those financial resources you've worked so hard to build up must now be converted to what is, in effect, your pension. For example, if you were an executive in a corporation instead of a business owner, part of your compensation package would likely include various programs designed for deferred consumption, such as a deferred profit-sharing plan, stock option plan, and a pension plan. In the case of an independent business owner or professional, it's our belief that the sum total of your investment assets, including registered plans, any proceeds from the sale of your business interests, RRSPs, and non-registered capital represents your pension. After all, these financial assets are for the most part meant to support you when you're no longer working and earning an income.

One of the primary reasons we believe it's worthwhile to start thinking about your investments as a pension is that it helps you to align your investment philosophies with the intended use of these assets. In the years leading up to your transition, you're in what could be thought of as an accumulation stage. This is an important step that we dealt with in earlier chapters. Once you complete your transition, you'll enter into a new phase of investment management, where the driving principles become both preservation of capital and income generation. Since time horizon plays an important role in strategies of this nature (this is explained later), we recommend that, depending on your circumstances, you start thinking of your investments as a pension well in advance of your intended transition date.

Experience has shown us that structuring your investment strategy similar to that of an institutionally managed pension plan has a high rate of success for busy entrepreneurs. What follows are comments, dos and don'ts, a case study, and recommended strategies that are appropriate for entrepreneurs and professionals within five years of their transition and beyond.

Case Study

To begin, let's relate a case from our files that can help illustrate the impact of investing on your transition plans. We met "Mike" in 2001, when he was fifty-one years old. He owned a productive and profitable business and wanted to plan his transition for some time in his late fifties, or at age sixty at the latest. Mike had been married to "Linda" for almost twenty-five years, and they had three children, one in university and two in high school.

While Mike had enjoyed a considerable income all his business life, a review of his financial affairs didn't reflect this. The RRSPs owned by him and his wife were not significant. There was comparatively little in the way of non-registered investments and they had a fair amount of debt. It was difficult to imagine where the money had gone. They had a nice house, yet it wasn't out of line for a family in their income bracket. Did they overspend on other lifestyle items? Did they give the money to charity? Did they gamble it away? No. It turns out the problem was investments.

As we talked about their finances, it became clear that over the years significant amounts of money had been lost on ill-considered investments. Mike had unsuccessfully "played the market," and had also bought a number of tax shelters, some of which had not only lost significant amounts but had been reassessed by the tax department. He also had a fair amount of investment-related debt. On the advice of his broker, he had borrowed money to invest in stocks during the heady days of the technology bubble. These funds had been invested in a limited number of speculative situations and had dropped precipitously once the bubble burst.

Mike's investment history indicated that he was a very aggressive investor. The problem, however, was that neither Mike nor his wife fully understood the risks involved, and they weren't "risk-takers" by nature. Actually, a risk assessment indicated that they had a conservative to moderate investment profile.

Mike is an intelligent and accomplished person in his profession, but like so many others, he had little training or experience to help him deal effectively in the investment arena. He didn't fully understand the risks he faced and how to manage them. He was also the victim of a system that in our view contains (and even promotes) a lot of myths and is rife with conflicts. A system that, outward appearances to the contrary, is not "investor friendly." Mike is not going to be able to reach his transition goals in the time frame he would have liked. But not to worry, he's just going to have to work a few more years. Had he invested more conservatively and not suffered such losses, our analysis indicated that he could have been in a position to work out of choice rather than necessity by his mid-fifties.

McNulty's Coaching Advice
Learn and adhere to the Twelve Principles of Investing for Entrepreneurs outlined below.

Twelve Principles of Investing for Entrepreneurs

After consulting with business owners for almost a quarter of a century on the management of their financial affairs, which by necessity includes their savings and investments, we've seen what works and what doesn't. Through this experience we've compiled a list of twelve principles we think you should consider for your pension (investment) program.

Principle One
The best investment most business owners will likely ever make is in their business itself. This is the source of their fiscal strength—it's what they're good at doing. The most successful transition strategies build on this fact by emphasizing preservation of capital as a primary objective for their passive investments and concentrating on generating wealth in the business. In other words, when it takes so much effort and energy to make the money intended to pay for your financial security and future financial freedom, *don't risk it.*

Principle Two

Risk and reward in the investment world are intimately linked. The bigger the return you want, the greater the risk you must undertake to earn it. In the investment world, risk is the premium you pay for greater returns. When making investment decisions, don't concentrate on return or potential return alone. Always consider the downside. Ask the "what if?" questions. Yes, all investments are subject to some form of risk or volatility. However, only undertake risk levels that are appropriate for your level of knowledge, risk tolerance, time horizons, investment objectives, and strategy. Perhaps the greatest risk to your investments is not having your money when you're going to need it!

Principle Three

It would be nice to think that your advisor (or anyone for that matter) knows what is likely to happen with interest rates, the economy, the stock market, and so on. But the simple fact is that no one knows for sure. If anyone knew what was likely to happen with a high degree of reliability, they would be rich beyond compare. Pick up any business paper and you'll see convincing articles and commentary from credible sources that purport to do just that—predict the future. Each of these articles supports their thesis with logic that sounds well thought out and researched. Yet such articles commonly express opinions that are completely opposite to opinions in other, equally scholarly writings. It can be confusing to say the least. Who do you believe? If you follow someone's recommendations and they're wrong, it's your money that will be lost, not theirs.

It most often takes a great deal of specialized training, experience, and education to be able to even hope to evaluate the wisdom of one investment opinion over another. Few busy entrepreneurs have the time for this. It's far better that you understand that no one can predict what's going to happen in the investment arena with any consistency. This insight is more potent because it will allow you to take a long-term view of your investments without being stressed by the "opinion de jour."

Market timing is one of the major reasons that many investors use the articles mentioned in the previous paragraphs. Study after study has shown, however, that neither pundits nor investors—even sophisticated ones—can effectively time the market consistently (i.e. pick the right time to go into the market and the right time to get out). Markets tend to move in spurts. Large changes can take place virtually in a single day. These moves happen so fast that it's impossible to consistently predict them in time. For example, if you had invested $1,000 in the S&P 500 (an American stock index) in 1951 and been able to predict when to get into the market and when to get out and been right 100% of the time, your $1,000 would have grown to $392,680,727 by the year 2000. That is a handsome sum by anyone's criteria. If you were right only 75% of the time, that $1,000 would have grown to $3,335,443. This is still a lot of money, but what a difference that 25% makes!

Interestingly, the next best alternative would have been to take a long-term view and not try to time the markets. In this case, your $1,000 would have grown to $56,851 in the time period. If you had been right only 50% of the time, your $1,000 would be worth less than half of what it would have been worth by staying invested all the time. If you were right only 25% of the time, you would have lost money! The economic, political, and investment worlds are just too complex to expect that you'll be able to make accurate market-timing decisions with the consistency required for success, particularly when you have an active business to run.

Let's look at another statistic. From January of 1990 to December of 2001, the Dow Jones average yearly return was 10.25%. If you guessed wrong and were out of this market during the best forty days (there were over four thousand days during this period), your return would have been a negative 0.49%. Similar studies have been done on the Toronto Stock Exchange (TSX) and the results have been the same. The top money managers in the world, trained and experienced professionals who have access to in-depth research material, cannot consistently time markets. Even if it was possible for you to consider market timing as part of your investment strategy, it would require a great deal of research to sort through the plethora of economic data that you would need to assess. In our experience, most independent business people are simply too busy to do this considering not only the demands of their enterprise but also family time and trying to have a personal life.

For the transitioning business owner, the most successful approach is to have a pension (investment) strategy in place that takes a long-term view, and no matter what happens, follow the plan. This might be challenging because things such as fear and greed influence our human emotions, but history has shown that this is your best option. When dealing with the financial members of your transition advisory team, insist on diversified strategies that aren't dependent on short-term trends or events for success.

Principle Four

The investment field is full of conflicts and it's important that you understand them. A few years ago, the U.S. Securities and Exchange Commission formed a committee on the future of the investment industry. It was called the Tulley Commission after Dan Tulley, who was chairman of Merrill Lynch at the time. This committee felt that the prevailing commission-based compensation system within the industry didn't provide value to investors. They went on to say that if they could redesign the business, it would be on a fee-based consultative process as opposed to the commission-driven transaction-based model. This is not to say that advisors who are compensated on a commission basis don't act ethically. Quite the contrary. There are many commission-based advisors who are professional and highly ethical. We have great empathy for anyone in the investment field who has to make their living on straight commission. There can be enormous pressures to trade actively. If they don't, how do they finance their lifestyle, pay for their children's education, the mortgage, and so on? Nonetheless, this can lead to the problem of not knowing whether a commission-compensated advisor is making recommendations motivated by what's in your best interests or by big commissions.

While we believe that working with a fee-for-service advisor is generally the best choice, it's important to keep in mind that conflicts exist in every business and profession. This applies to fee-based investment arrangements as well. Just because you are paying a fee, be it an hourly rate, a flat fee, or a percentage of assets, it is in your best interests to make sure you understand them. For example, where possible, work with a fee-for-service advisor who has access to all forms of investments, not just proprietary products.

Principle Five

Whether you are dealing with a fee-for-service or commission-driven advisor, it's important to make sure they're qualified. Someone wanting to become a broker in Canada today needs only to pass the Canadian Securities Course (CSC), taken by correspondence, and fulfill some other regulatory requirements such as passing the Conduct and Practices Handbook (CPH) exam and registering with the appropriate securities and industry regulators. The CSC, offered by the Canadian Securities Institute, is a good basic course. But that's all it is.

You should, however, be dealing with someone who has more qualifications than just the basics. Having an MBA, an accounting designation, or even a Ph.D. doesn't necessarily mean the person has advanced training in the investment world. Look for a combination of related designations. The CFP (Certified Financial Planner) is a desirable designation and provides training for working with a client's overall financial circumstances. Your investment portfolio isn't a stand-alone aspect of your finances in the same way that your leg isn't separate from the rest of your body. Integration is very important. Someone with a CFP must also adhere to a strict code of ethics and standards. In addition, CFPs are required to obtain a minimum of thirty hours of education credits per year to keep their knowledge-base current.

In addition to the CSC and CFP, an advisor needs more advanced training on investment. A CIM (Certified Investment Manager) or CFA (Certified Financial Analyst) designation is a good indication that an advisor has furthered their education in investment management and strategies. There are many other designations that an advisor can earn, and the effort they have put into acquiring advanced specialized qualifications is a good indication of their abilities. We should point out that there's a lot of controversy within the financial community on qualifications. Some argue that there are designations and qualifications that are as good as the CFP, and they could be right, but we have very little personal knowledge of these other courses.

The point we are making here is that it's the combination of the CSC, CFP, and CIM or CFA—as opposed to any one designation—that's a good indicator of who is and who isn't qualified to be the investment member of your transition advisory team. We must admit that we possess some of these designations and have something of a conflict of interest or bias in this area. The bias is intentional. We have spent a lot of time researching what courses of study provide the best tools for working with clients on their financial affairs.

Principle Six

Choosing to work with an advisor that has a desirable combination of qualifications is only part of the job. We believe that the best way to work with any advisor is to delegate the investment management of your portfolio as opposed to abdicating authority over it. After all, this is your money and your future. You have a right to ask a lot of questions. It's important you understand and agree with the strategy and feel that it fits well with your overall transition planning. If you don't understand it, don't invest in it. If your advisor can't explain it to your satisfaction, well that should be an indication.

Principle Seven

Manage on a portfolio basis as opposed to an asset-by-asset basis. This relates back to the earlier comment that no one knows what's going to happen in the future. Diversification is an excellent way of dealing with this fact. If done properly, a portfolio should include a mix of assets that react differently to economic, political, and market conditions. At any one time, some assets might be up, while others might be down. By managing on a portfolio basis, you place the emphasis on obtaining the overall yield or return you need at the risk level that's appropriate to your circumstances. There are a couple of books you might want to review that can give you some more insight on this topic. They are *Risk is Still a Four Letter Word* by George Hartman and *Secrets of Successful Investing* by Gordon Pape and Eric Kirzner.

Principle Eight

Over the last few years, short-term volatility has increased dramatically. If you can't invest for the long term, only put your money into something safe and sure. Consider, for example, T-bills, GICs, or government bonds with a weighted maturity under five years. Otherwise, you might find that you need to cash in investments that are volatile in nature at the wrong time, when things are down. It's a proven fact that time horizon plays a critical role in investment success.

Principle Nine

Don't look at your portfolio in isolation. In the investment world, everything is relative. In demonstrating this point to clients, we often ask the question, "In a given year is an 8% return good or bad?" The answer depends on comparisons. If an investment with a similar level of risk earned 6% during the same period, it's a great return. On the other hand, if another comparable investment earned 10% then the 8% result isn't that good. A practical resource for making such comparisons are the various indexes that are published in any reputable business publication and on certain Internet sites.

Principle Ten

Don't take risks with the fixed income (bonds, guaranteed investment certificates, mortgage backed securities, and so on) component of your portfolio. The importance of diversification was mentioned earlier. Each investment strategy should contain some fixed income, which is the component of your portfolio that represents a stabilizing force for your investment strategy. Most people are unaware that fixed income is subject to a number of different types of risk.

One key type is interest-rate risk. If you had a thirty-year Government of Canada bond in your portfolio, paying say 6%, and interest rates increased so that bonds of similar credit risk and term were earning 8%, what do you think would happen to the resale value of your bond? It would dramatically drop in value. Who's going to pay you one hundred cents on the dollar for your bond to get a 6% rate of return when they can buy someone else's for the same price and get 8%? The only way you could sell that bond is if the price was adjusted downward so that the 6% on the face of the bond equalled 8% on the actual price the purchaser paid.

McNulty's Coaching Advice

Invest in high-quality credit risks only and keep your average maturity to five years (shorter maturities are less sensitive to interest-rate volatility).

Principle Eleven

If you're considering mutual funds or some other form of managed money concept such as working with an investment counsellor, exclude compound performance from your selection criteria. It can be very misleading. Let's say you were evaluating a mutual fund that had been in existence for three years. The first year it made 50%. The second year it lost 5% and the third year it lost 15%. Obviously, this is not a good trend. Yet its compound rate of return would still be 10% per year.

Year-by-year performance statistics are readily available and they can give you a clear picture of the track record of the particular investment vehicle you're considering. They also make comparisons with similar managers and appropriate indexes much easier. However, don't buy last year's winner. If a mutual fund or a particular sector of the market did really well last year, don't kick yourself for not buying in earlier and try to quickly remedy the situation.

If a stock or mutual fund drastically exceeded general market performance in a given year, statistics show that buying it now is likely not a good decision. Chances are you'll be either too late and performance from here on in will be lacklustre or you could even incur a loss. The old expression "what goes up must come down" very often applies to last year's top performers in the investment world!

In addition, don't invest in a mutual fund that has a track record that is less than three years old. To make an informed decision, you need to compare the performance of the fund to similar funds and to appropriate indexes. A lot has been written about management expense ratios (MER). They can reduce your effective returns if the performance isn't there to justify the cost or if you're not getting value for your money. When you buy a mutual fund, you're effectively hiring a supposedly experienced investment manager. Without access to at least three years of performance criteria on that particular fund, how are you to make an assessment?

The sales pitch on new mutual funds often relates to the great track record of a manager who worked on another fund or fund family. You can't rely on this. The previous company could have had a different decision-making process, more or less supervision, better or worse research capabilities, and a variety of other factors that could influence performance.

Principle Twelve: Our final guideline would be to understand the many risks you face as an investor: some of them aren't always that obvious.

Types of Risks you Face as an Investor

Systematic Risk (sometimes called market risk) can affect all portfolios regardless of quality. Many people think of market risk as exclusively applying to the stock market, but it's important to recognize that this also applies to the fixed-income market. Systematic risk addresses movements in broad markets. You could own the best in blue chip stocks but if the market declines as a whole, then the value of all stocks will decline. Similarly, if the broad market increases, those blue chip stocks would likely increase in value right along with the rest. The point here is that these movements have nothing to do with the specific investment. The volatility actually relates to factors that affect various markets as a whole, such as good or bad economic news. Unfortunately, owning blue chip stocks won't protect your portfolio from unwanted volatility.

Systematic risk is one of the reasons why you need to diversify your portfolio. Different types of assets such as stocks, cash or near cash (money markets, T-bills), fixed income, and so on. don't necessarily react in the same way to outside stimuli. When the stock market declines, it's not uncommon to see an improvement in fixed-income assets. This is because general markets work somewhat on a supply and demand basis. When stock markets start to decline, investors fear they will lose money and demand is reduced. In times of uncertainty, investors often look for security. In doing this, much of the money from the sale of stocks is put into fixed-income alternatives, thereby increasing demand. They don't perfectly offset each other, but having your portfolio diversified between types of assets can help ease volatility.

Unsystematic Risk (or company specific risk) represents another reason that you should manage your investments on a portfolio basis and diversify your portfolio. Think about the once great companies that have fallen on hard times. We've all heard the old adage "Don't put all your eggs in one basket." That concept definitely applies here. While opinions differ, many investment professionals believe you need somewhere between twenty and thirty or even more companies in a stock portfolio to properly address unsystematic risk.

To add additional protection against volatility, these companies should be diversified by industry (it's possible for an entire industry to go into a slump) and geographic location. Choosing the appropriate companies for such a portfolio demands a lot of expertise and hard work. Think about the information you would want to see when buying another ongoing business, perhaps a business totally unrelated to the one you're in now, for cash. You would need details on financial performance, costs, service or product mix, employees, and on and on. When you're adding a company to your portfolio, you're fundamentally buying a business. To make sure you're making the right decision, you should do a thorough analysis of the company in question. You'll also have to monitor it on an ongoing basis. The fact that it takes so much effort is one of the reasons why mutual funds and managed investment alternatives are popular.

Inflation risk (or risk to your spending power) must also be addressed. This is particularly true when you're constructing a portfolio while contemplating your succession. You could be living off that portfolio longer than you had actually worked!

If today you spend $75,000 per year after tax to maintain your lifestyle, then ten years from now, at 3% inflation, you'll need $100,793 to buy the same goods and services. In twenty years, you'll need $135,458. The best way to deal with inflation is to have a component within your pension, if you will, that will grow on an after-tax basis at a rate that is higher than inflation. This is one of the main reasons you need a well-designed pension (investment) strategy. If it wasn't for the long-term negative effects of inflation, you could leave all your money in assets that are very safe and sure such as treasury bills. When tax and inflation are considered, treasury bills can often experience negative real growth—in other words, lose purchasing power.

Exchange rate risk is another possible area of volatility. During the summer of 2003, the U.S. greenback substantially declined in value relative to the Canadian dollar. If, at that time, you had all or substantially all of your transition assets denominated in U.S. dollars, their current value would have declined dramatically. Once again, being diversified is the answer.

Credit risk is similar to unsystematic risk in that it's company specific. In this case, it applies to fixed income. Governments and corporations, including financial institutions such as banks, issue debt of various kinds. Credit risk for governments in Canada and the United States are generally thought to be very low.

In Canada, when dealing with the credit risk on bank deposits and securities such as GICs, you don't need to be concerned about any credit risk up to $60,000 because of the guarantee of the Canada Deposit Insurance Corporation (CDIC). Other debt, such as corporate debt, might not be as secure. Fortunately, there are ratings on most debt available from such companies as the Dominion Bond Rating Service and Moodys that will give you guidance for your decisions.

Political risk can also affect your portfolio. We're not just talking about things like the September 11th attack in the United States. Regulatory changes can also have a serious effect on some industries. Political interference is another concern. An example is the National Energy Program in Canada, which ultimately resulted in investors in the oil and gas sector experiencing significant declines in share values.

Additional Risks Faced by Entrepreneurs
Management Time

We've seen a number of clients with very successful businesses who have decided they would invest in something that required active management—frequently being rental real estate. One client bought into a small company started by a long-time friend and associate. The original deal was that there would be no management time required by our client (incidentally, he became a client well after acquiring his interest in this company). Unfortunately, things did not go very well. Not only did the friendship run into problems but the client also had to step in and start taking an active role in the business. He had a large part of his Net Worth tied up in this company so if he didn't devote his time there was a risk that his investment would be lost. When reviewing his business' financial statements from a number of years, it was easy to identify the exact year he had to start devoting time to this company.

In the end, the investment didn't make money and the hidden cost was the loss of income from the operating business. Income declined because the client's focus was elsewhere. Direct ownership of real estate can also have a material drain on your available time. Negotiating rents, collecting rents, maintenance, repairs, dealing with mortgages, and everything else involved can take a large part of your emotional energy. This energy would probably be more profitable if devoted to your business.

The Possibility of Making a Costly Error
It would be foolish to treat yourself for a serious illness or look after your own dental health. We don't have the training or the experience to be a physician or dentist. Similarly, it takes many years of education, experience, and training to become an investment professional.

As an exception to the rule, there are people who do a good job managing their own investments. In our experience, these success stories fall into two categories. In the first category, the person is very interested in the investment process, works hard at it, has educated themselves, and has gained valuable experience. In the other case, the individual recognizes their limitations and works with a simple investment strategy, where management fits into their schedule.

In the investment world there's something called the efficient market hypothesis. This theory contends that all information generally available to the investing public has already been factored into the price of a particular asset such as a stock or mutual fund. There is naturally some controversy surrounding the validity of the efficient market hypothesis, but a number of studies seem to support it. Even those who don't agree with it acknowledge that in general, it takes a lot of work and investment know-how to identify undervalued opportunities in advance of the market. For busy entrepreneurs who aren't investment professionals, we believe it's reasonable to accept the efficient market hypothesis and invest for the long term.

The Risk of Not Having Your Money When You Need It

Many business owners have aggressive investments in their portfolios. As mentioned earlier in this chapter, risk and reward are intimately linked. The greater the reward you try to achieve, the greater the risk you must undertake to obtain that reward. That's the trade off. It's something of a conundrum. You want to invest aggressively to grow your assets as much as possible, yet because of the increased risk, you endanger your financial security. If you end up losing money, it's extremely hard to make it back.

The place to create wealth is in your business, and the purpose of Wealth Management is first to hang onto the wealth you create and second to obtain a reasonable rate of real growth (after tax and inflation).

The Need for a Formal Pension (Investment) Strategy

One of the key reasons you need to have a formal investment strategy is to help you manage the many risks you face. A cornerstone of modern portfolio theory is diversification. Harry Markowitz, a Nobel Prize-winning mathematician, proved it was possible to reduce risks and in some cases simultaneously improve returns through diversification. Another mathematician, Gary Brinson, named in 1993 one of the four most influential investors in the world, found that the most important contributor to investment success wasn't asset selection (what stocks to pick, etc.) or market timing, but rather the decision to diversify. He found that the decision to diversify contributed an overwhelming 90% to investment success. Later studies have supported these conclusions and in some cases attributed even greater weight to the decision of asset allocation. By the way, "asset allocation" is the buzzword within the investment community applied to the concept of planned diversification in the construction of investment strategies.

Another benefit of using a formal investment strategy is that it helps to take the emotion out of investing. Emotions such as fear of loss or desire for additional profits can have a material impact on such questions as "When should I buy?", "Is a 5% return satisfactory?", "Should I hold on until the return goes up to 10% or 15% or more?", "When is the right time to sell an investment that has experienced a loss?" These are difficult questions. Ideally, investing should be a methodical, disciplined process that demands a formal strategy approach.

Finally, a formal investment strategy helps you monitor results and make appropriate and timely adjustments to your portfolio. When you prepare your investment strategy, expectations are established such as the expected range of return and volatility level. Once you have reasonable expectations, the actual performance of the strategy can be compared with those expectations. It also becomes possible to gauge the strategy's performance by comparing it to appropriate benchmarks or indexes. Being able to monitor results and make appropriate comparisons is really the essence of control.

Establishing Your Investment Strategy

First let's summarize the principles or rules of investing that in our experience work best for entrepreneurs, as defined earlier:

- Recognize that Wealth Creation is an active business activity, while Wealth Management is what your investment strategy should do.
- Keep in mind that risk and reward are linked. The higher the reward, the higher the risk.
- Remember that no one knows what's going to happen in the future. You'll be faced with many risks as an investor. Diversification is the key, so that no matter what happens there is a higher expectation you'll have your money when you need it.
- Studies show that market timing does not work consistently.
- The investment world is full of conflicts. Make sure you understand them before making your investment decisions.
- If an investment professional is a member of your advisory team, make sure they are properly qualified and, if possible, deal with someone who works on a fee-for-service basis.
- If a qualified investment professional is a member of your transition advisory team, delegate but don't abdicate.
- Manage your assets on a portfolio basis as opposed to asset by asset. Nothing will ever be up or down all the time. The trick is to build your portfolio with assets that complement or offset each other.
- Invest for the long term.
- Don't look at individual investments or your portfolio in isolation. Compare performance to appropriate benchmarks.
- Don't take risks with the fixed-income portion of your portfolio. Invest in high-quality credit risks, vary your

maturities so that you are reinvesting approximately 20% of your fixed-income portfolio every year, and keep the weighted average maturities of your fixed-income assets to five years or under.

- Don't use compound rates of return as performance criteria in your specific asset selection process; year-by-year performance is much more useful. Also, look for consistent performance instead of chasing last year's big winners.

Asset Allocation and Your Investment Strategy

There's an order to the way one should formulate an investment strategy. Many books written about investing start with establishing specific goals then continue with a discussion on determining risk tolerance levels followed by a discussion on the importance of time horizons. We're going to diverge from this standard because this book is on transition planning for independent business owners and professionals and therefore not general in nature. Also, chapter one is devoted to goal setting, so let's start by assuming that your goals are already in place and your risk tolerance level is conservative. The first step is to decide how your assets will be diversified—the asset allocation plan—for your portfolio. Listed below are the three broad asset classes from which to choose, along with what we would consider to be their risk profile:

- Cash (bank deposits, T-bills) or near cash (secure money markets, Government of Canada bonds with a maturity under one year). (Low risk)
- Fixed-income investments, such as GICs or bonds, with quality credit risks and an average maturity of five years or under. (Low to moderate risk)
- Diversified portfolio of equities. (Moderate to high risk on holding periods, or time horizons, of less than five to ten years)

Having dealt with all of the above, you now have two choices: you can establish your plan yourself or you can make a qualified investment professional a member of your transition advisory team. Our advice, frankly, would be to hire a professional to help with the design of the strategy even if you want to manage it yourself. For those who are establishing their own investment strategy, be sure to pick up a good book on the topic. We mentioned a couple earlier in this chapter.

If you're working with an advisor, make sure they put forth enough time and effort to gain a complete understanding of your overall financial circumstances, your goals, risk tolerance levels, time horizons, and other constraints, if any. Your investment professional should be able to demonstrate how the recommended asset allocation model has performed historically over the last one-, three-, five-, ten-, and fifteen-year periods. Databases are readily available to investment professionals for this purpose. Also, ask that the performance of the proposed asset allocation model be compared in a graph format, for the periods mentioned above, against appropriate indexes so that you can see how it performed on a comparative basis.

After your advisor has produced an asset allocation model that is to your satisfaction, it's necessary to pick the specific assets that will populate the various categories in your model. The selection criteria should be governed by the fact that you'll be monitoring the portfolio's performance relative to the indexes. Your expectation is that your portfolio will do as well as or better than the portfolio of indexes. If the assets in the various categories do not perform as well as the index, then this is an indication that a change is necessary. In many cases, it might just be prudent to buy the indexes themselves. This can be done with mutual funds that replicate the indexes or with instruments such as iUnits (the Canadian member of the global family of exchange-traded funds from Barclays Global Investors).

Monitoring Your Investment Strategy and Ongoing Rebalancing

Your asset allocation will have to be rebalanced regularly, and we recommend quarterly. This is important because change is inevitable. Let's say that in one quarter your Canadian equity component had gone up dramatically. It's supposed to represent 10% of your portfolio under your asset allocation plan. Now, as a result of this increase, it represents 20%. This is what's called "portfolio drift." If you don't sell off 10% of those equities and redistribute the monies into the other categories so the portfolio is brought back into line with the allocation plan, you will lose control of your strategy and can no longer expect that it will perform in the manner for which it was designed.

There's another advantage in rebalancing. Most investors sell low and buy high. In effect, this system of management attempts to reverse that process. When one area of the portfolio is up, a portion of it must be sold and the funds invested in an area that's down. This system helps to provide you with the discipline necessary to have you selling high and buying low.

In addition to rebalancing on a quarterly basis, we recommend you have your investment professional prepare a comparison showing how the various indexes representing your asset allocation model performed in the same period. Did you do better, worse, or the same? If you did better or the same, then it's reasonable to assume the strategy is working as anticipated during the period under review. If it didn't perform as well, you should be able to determine why. You'll then need to make a decision about whether it's necessary to change some of the specific holdings that make up your asset category in order to achieve the performance you expect and want.

Chapter Ten
Risk Management

This chapter will help you:
* **Develop a philosophy to guide your insurance strategies,**
* **Understand the various types of insurance and assess your need for coverage,**
* **See the benefits of business contingency planning, including business or office overhead insurance, and**
* **Understand other important information related to this topic.**

Given time and proper planning, most established business owners have the *potential* to build a relative level of financial security and success. We emphasize the word *potential* because, as the saying goes, "Life is what happens while you're making other plans." Unfortunately, this means that in any population group, statistics show that a certain percentage of people will experience some form of calamity for which the financial consequences are significant. Such calamities happen at random and can affect anyone. Now, chances are you'll be one of the lucky ones but there's no way to be absolutely sure. Some catastrophe could happen to you, your business, or a member of your family. It's only prudent, therefore, that your transition strategies include planning for such contingencies.

Risk management is a very important topic, yet there's

a lot of confusion concerning how to go about formulating appropriate, coordinated strategies. This is particularly true of risk management strategies that involve insurance, so it's our hope that this chapter will help to clarify this important topic.

Why It's Important to Establish Your Own Philosophy About Insurance

Insurance can be both complex and expensive. Worse than that, insurance policies can be pretty dull to read. These complicated, difficult to understand contracts create a barrier that can reduce the ability of busy entrepreneurs to be informed consumers of insurance products. Also, there are so many insurance products available that it can feel as if there are a limitless number of variations. Who has the time or legal training to read all these contracts and fully understand the benefits of one variation over another?

Insurance can also be a major expense, particularly as most premiums have to be paid from after-tax dollars. And if you never have to make a claim, paying them can feel like a waste of money. So, where is the satisfaction from paying that expensive premium? You don't get much in the way of "pizzazz" for your insurance dollar. It's not like you can reach out and touch it, put it in your living room and admire it, or take it for a spin on a pleasant summer day. In addition, your resources are finite, which means that if you spend money on insurance coverage you don't really need, those funds won't be available for other important things in life.

There are also many potential conflicts in the way insurance is sold in Canada today. Don't misunderstand. There are many capable and ethical insurance agents in the marketplace, and we have respect for what they do. It's only that these potential conflicts are one more reason why it's important that you establish your own insurance philosophy. It's the only way you can hope to control the process and be sure that you're getting value for the money you put towards premiums.

How to Establish Your Insurance Philosophy

Start with the premise that the purpose of insurance is first and foremost to protect you against being one who is hurt by life's random events. Next, adopt the KIS principle— "Keep it Simple." Perhaps we can explain more effectively what we mean by relating this philosophy to the experience of buying a car. You can purchase a luxury vehicle with all the bells and whistles or, if you simply want basic transportation, you can buy a less expensive automobile that still does the job of getting you from point A to point B.

When you apply this example to insurance, paying that extra money for the luxury model won't give you the pleasure that you would get from a fully loaded, luxury automobile. Of course, it's ultimately up to you. In our view, it makes good sense philosophically to concentrate on acquiring and maintaining insurance coverage that takes you from A to B. This means insuring risks with the simplest alternatives possible. We're talking about risks you can't afford to underwrite yourself. Now having said all that, we do believe that insurance is a necessity, and we don't mean to imply that you should buy only the cheapest available. Assessing your need is an individual process. Once you've decided on your insurance philosophy, it's important to communicate it to your agents when considering a proposal or obtaining quotes. Get competing quotations (not from the same agent, even if they state that they can survey all the insurance companies for the best product). Finally, insist that as part of the quotation the agent shows you how their proposal complies with your philosophical approach to insurance.

Case Study

One of our clients has seen his business income grow dramatically over the last couple of years. Given this higher income, his insurance agent felt that he should increase his disability insurance and provided him with a proposal. If the client went ahead, it would mean a significant increase in the annual premium.

By way of background, this client is in good financial shape. He and his wife have always had a lifestyle that costs significantly less than their income. As a result, they have no debt and have accumulated a sizable investment portfolio. My client's definition of the risk of disability was not being able to provide for his current lifestyle needs and future financial security.

After reviewing the proposal with the client and relating it to his unique financial picture, we recommended that he decline the offer of additional coverage. He was in complete agreement that he didn't need to spend money insuring his income. The fact was that he already had sufficient disability coverage to provide for his wants and his current lifestyle needs. Further analysis indicated, with a high level of confidence, that his portfolio was sufficient to provide for his retirement needs if it was left to grow until he was sixty-five. Age sixty-five is when his disability benefit would run out in the case of a claim. His present coverage would be adequate to provide for his lifestyle before retirement and he already had a nest egg for the future. It was even decided that we would change the elimination period on his policy from sixty days to a much longer period. This reduced his current premium. He had the cash reserves to handle a short-term disability so in effect he was paying for coverage he didn't need.

Life Insurance

Of the various types of insurance you might require, the most fundamental is life insurance. Ben Feldman, a famous insurance man with New York Life Insurance Company, once said, "The basic purpose of life insurance is to create cash...nothing more...and nothing less." Should the person insured under the contract die, the insurance company pays out cash either to the named beneficiaries or to the estate. To determine how much insurance you need, keep in mind that life insurance for business owners is typically required to produce cash for the following risks:

• Ongoing lifestyle needs for your spouse and family,
• Funding your children's education,
• Retiring outstanding debt,
• Providing funding to surviving shareholders, partners, cost-sharing associates, or members of your self-protection group (applicable for certain professional practices) to purchase your business interests,
• Paying for taxes as a result of the insured's demise (capital gains, recapture),
• Covering estate legal and administrative needs,
• Leaving a specified sum for your heirs, and
• Leaving money to a charity or religious group.

How Much Coverage Do You Need?

Some people feel that you can never have too much life insurance. Interestingly, most of the people who feel this way are insurance agents. You can't blame them for being enthusiastic about what they sell. However, you'll have to decide what's right for your own circumstances.

Our recommendation, as mentioned above, is that you buy enough life insurance to cover the risks that you don't have the ability to underwrite yourself. This means you have to work out or effectively quantify those risks with a financial member of your transition advisory team (not someone who's selling you insurance) prior to meeting with your insurance agent.

Three Steps for Working Out Your Need for Life Insurance

1. *Estimate your needs today.*
   Specifically, make estimates on:
- Final expenses such as funeral and burial costs,
- Paying off all debt, including business loans and leases,
- Emergency cash needs of your family until insurance is paid out and the estate settled,
- Tax,
- Total education costs for your children,
- Living costs of your spouse and family until your spouse's retirement and other family members are independent,
- How much capital your spouse will need to finance his or her retirement, and
- The amount you would like to leave to charity, religious affiliations, or other estate wishes, such as leaving a specific amount to your heirs, providing money to keep the cottage in the family, and so on.

2. *Estimate what you already have to meet those needs.*
   Specifically, make estimates on:
- Investment assets such as RRSPs and savings of both spouses,
- Cash or near-cash reserves,
- Income your surviving spouse might expect to earn,
- Insurance already in place, and
- The tangible assets of the business on a distress sale basis unless a solid buy/sell agreement is in place where the formula would incorporate a fair value for goodwill.

3. *Deduct the total you arrived at from your calculations in step 2 from the needs you worked out in step 1.*
   A deficit should equal the amount of insurance coverage you need. If there's a surplus, you'll have to decide whether or not you're getting value for such coverage. We

find that many of our clients, as they approach transition, become self-insured.

This analysis should be performed for both husband and wife, as well as for an event of joint disaster, to make sure your needs and wishes are addressed for any eventuality.

Types of Life Insurance

Generally, life insurance falls into two broad categories: term insurance and permanent insurance. The two are quite different. It might help to think of the differences in the following way: with term insurance, you're basically renting the coverage you need, and with permanent life insurance, you're buying it.

1. Term Insurance

Term insurance provides coverage for a specific period of time such as five, ten, or twenty years or to age one hundred. At the end of that period, the policy and any applicable renewals will expire without any cash value. Generally, this form of life insurance is less expensive when you're younger and increases in cost as you age. We find it particularly well suited for many of our clients because they typically need the largest amount of coverage at the time when the most demands are being made on their Cash Flow.

In examining a client's insurance needs, we often find they resemble a bell curve on a chart. For example, when their family is young, debts tend to be heavy because of the long period of support that must be provided—they're paying off their home and establishing their business, etc. As they age, debts decline, the amount of time they have to provide for the lifestyle needs of their surviving spouse and children is reduced, and their assets build. Eventually, it's possible that their assets will grow to the point that they become self-insured from a risk of premature death.

As an aside, we often wonder why the insurance industry doesn't refer to term to 100 as permanent insurance. It certainly seems like permanent coverage. The only difference is that it doesn't build up cash surrender value, but it also costs a whole lot less.

McNulty's Coaching Advice

When buying term insurance, two options (bells and whistles) we'd recommend are:
1. It should be guaranteed renewable without evidence of insurability to eliminate the concern over renewing coverage if there's been a change in your health.
2. It should be guaranteed convertible in case you should come to need permanent coverage for some reason in the future.

2. *Permanent Insurance*

Permanent insurance is intended to provide coverage for your entire life. It's often referred to as "whole life." A popular variation of permanent insurance is called "universal life." There are two components to this form of life insurance. One is the insurance coverage and the other is a savings component.

Permanent insurance generally involves a level premium either for your whole life or for a specific period of time, such as twenty years. Typically, these costs are significantly higher than comparable term coverage when you're young. At some point as you get older, there's a crossover where the annual premium cost for term coverage becomes greater than the level premium of the permanent policy alternative. When making a choice between permanent coverage and term coverage, we've often heard the argument made by insurance agents that the level premium permanent coverage is actually cheaper because of the high cost of maintaining a term policy in later life.

If you want to compare the cost of term versus level premium permanent coverage, have your financial advisor (not the one selling the insurance contract) do a "present value" analysis of the two premium payment streams. This is a mainstream form of financial analysis that compares different future inflows (the future cash surrender value) and outflows (the premiums, etc.). The premise behind this form of analysis is that a dollar today is worth much more than a dollar in the future. For example, at 3% inflation, a dollar payable twenty years from now is really worth about 55¢ in present-value terms. Think of it this way: a present-value analysis is a way of converting an apples-to-oranges comparison to an apples-to-apples comparison when cost alone is your main criterion. The alternative with the greatest present-value cost, provided you are comfortable with the assumptions used (e.g. inflation, investment returns, and so on), is the most expensive. Also, if there is ever a possibility that you will be self-insured at some point in the future, you would have to question the value of paying high premium costs today when you most likely need the money for other important things, and so that you will have life insurance in the future. Keep in mind that there is an option with term coverage that gives you the right to convert to permanent coverage, so you do have an alternative if things don't work out the way you think they will. Of course, you could face higher premiums if you convert in the future, so you might want to do a present-value comparison on this scenario as well.

Permanent insurance might be a better choice than term coverage for the following reasons:

- *You expect to have income tax arising on death*

Upon your death, there's a deemed disposition of all your assets. Depending on the makeup of your Net Worth, this would typically mean tax on any capital gains existing at the time of your passing and tax from having all of your RRSPs or RRIFs deemed as income at that point. In Canada there are regulatory provisions that allow, on the death of one spouse, for non-registered assets to be transferred to the surviving spouse at the adjusted cost base of the deceased. Likewise, there are spousal rollover provisions for your RRSP (your spouse should be the named beneficiary for your RRSPs, and it's also a good idea to include a clause to that effect in your will).

These rollover provisions allow the surviving spouse to transfer any RRSP or RRIF assets directly into their own plans without paying any immediate tax. The result is that tax on capital gains or on RRSP assets can be effectively deferred until the passing of the surviving spouse. This leaves three potential scenarios where you might want to consider permanent life insurance to pay tax upon death:

1. You're single and want to preserve the pre-tax value of your estate.
2. You're married and want to preserve the pre-tax value of your estate, consider the permanent policy on a "joint last to die" basis, where both spouses are covered and the insurance benefits aren't paid until the death of the surviving spouse. The premiums are often less expensive with this type of policy.
3. You have an asset such as a family cottage that you want to make sure remains in your family and a significant capital gain has built up. Once again, because of the spousal rollover provisions you might want to consider such coverage on a "joint last to die" basis.

• *Savings in a permanent insurance policy can grow tax-free*
One of the selling points often promoted as a reason to buy permanent insurance is the potential for tax-free growth of the cash surrender value (CSV). Provided the amount of insurance relative to the investment component of the policy is in compliance with a government formula, the investment component grows tax-free. Both insurance companies and agents enthusiastically promote this fea-

ture. For many entrepreneurs who typically carry more than their proportional share of the Canadian tax burden, such a feature might be music to your ears. You should, however, take a close look before you sign.

After policy taxes, administration charges, selling costs, high management fees for some of their investment alternatives, and the cost of the insurance, the tax-free benefit might not be so great. This is particularly true when the investment growth is compared to other alternatives, even when you factor in the tax. Many permanent life insurance contracts are sold with the idea that the policyholder will use the built-up CSV in retirement as security for a loan to generate non-taxable Cash Flow. The most common type of permanent insurance we've seen used on this basis is referred to as universal life. Normally, if you withdraw funds from the CSV of your universal life policy, it will attract some tax. However, there's no income tax on borrowed money.

The idea is that the policy is assigned to the bank as security for the funds you have borrowed. When you die, the benefits are paid to the bank. The bank then uses the proceeds to pay off any outstanding loans plus accumulated interest. There's no tax on life insurance benefits. The balance of the benefits is then paid to your estate or heirs. This is a great concept in theory, and we've analyzed many universal life proposals for our clients. Unfortunately, when you cut through all the fancy sales material, there are very few that we're prepared to recommend.

One common problem is with the assumptions used to illustrate the potential advantages of the policy. In our experience, they're often not appropriate and the illustrations are often confusing. So before proceeding with such a strategy, have it analyzed by a financial member of your transition advisory team who is familiar with these types of policies—someone who has no connection with the agent selling the insurance. In particular, make sure the analysis is done on a comparative basis, because there are other assets that can compound on a tax-free basis. For example, compare it to putting the money into an investment such as an exchange traded fund or into certain types of mutual funds that can be tax-efficient.

There are a number of concerns with the leveraging strategy, whether you're borrowing against an insurance policy or a non-registered asset. If you're considering such a strategy, be sure to explore both the pros and cons of the equation.

• *A special need exists*

An example of a special need might be if you have a special child who, after you're gone, won't be able to provide for themselves financially. In this case, we recommend you talk to your lawyer or estate planner about the potential benefits of a permanent life insurance contract in combination with a "Henson trust" (in Ontario, a trust worded so that a child with disabilities is deemed not to have personally received the inheritance). Depending on the circumstances, it might be possible to leave the insurance policy to such a trust without affecting your child's right to certain government benefits.

• *You want to leave a specific amount to your heirs, a charity, a religious affiliation, or for some other special purpose*

This is an individual choice, for the most part. If you're interested in leaving funds to a charity or religious affiliation through an insurance policy of this type, there are some specialized tax benefits you might want to check into.

Disability Insurance

Disability insurance is very expensive, so it's important to make sure that you have the right amount of coverage for your unique circumstances. Generally, insurance companies will cover you to a maximum of 60 to 70% of your pre-tax income, so you'll have to decide what needs you want to cover with this insurance. Do you want to insure your income or do you want to insure your lifestyle and obligations? One could be much higher than the other.

We feel that you'll get the most value for the money you spend on disability coverage by matching it to needs you can't afford to underwrite yourself. The following is the form of analysis we would use to determine our own optimum disability insurance level:

Add
• An estimate of your annual personal lifestyle costs.
• All payment obligations.
• Savings needs for the children's education.
• Savings needs for retirement.
• Fixed costs and Cash Flow commitments in your business.

Deduct
• Spouse's salary if he or she will continue to work. Note that if your spouse works for your business, you will have to consider how viable the business will be if you are unable to work. In many cases, your disability could result in your spouse eventually being unemployed.
• Ongoing business income, assuming you are confident it will operate profitably in your absence.
• Investment income.
• Business overhead insurance. Be sure you understand exactly what it will cover. One area to look at in particular is whether it will cover debt service for the business. Another question to consider is whether it will cover the cost of your spouse's salary.

Definitions of Disability

One of the most important things to understand about the policy you buy is the definition of 'disability.' The tighter the definition is, the more expensive the coverage because there is a greater risk that the insurance company will have to pay out a benefit. For example, some policies may provide benefits if you're unable to perform the regular duties of your own occupation. Other policies state that you would only be considered disabled if you were unable to work at any job. The policy may also include a provision to provide benefits if you suffer a loss of income of say 20% or more. Some policies have stringent definitions of disability or partial disability, while others are more broadly defined. It's important that you check the terms of the contract being proposed to you (or the one you currently have in place) to make sure you're comfortable with the definition of disability.

Elimination Period

This is the length of time you must be disabled before you're eligible to collect the benefits. Typically you have the option of choosing fifteen, thirty, sixty, ninety, or 180 days. The shorter the elimination period is, the higher the premium. Remember that you'll get the greatest value from your insurance expenditures by insuring against risks that you can't afford to cover yourself. Many business people don't need to spend the money to have a fifteen-day elimination period. You could be off that long with a bad flu virus. During that period, the business could easily continue to operate and earn profits. You may also have cash reserves or accounts receivable which would provide for your cash needs during this period.

We'd recommend you determine how long you could be away from work before it becomes a serious financial setback, and then structure your elimination period accordingly.

McNulty's Coaching Advice
You might be able to save money by breaking up your policies with a variety of elimination periods, depending on how you assess your individual needs.

The Benefit Period

Typically, the longer the benefit period is, the higher the premium. It's worthwhile to carefully consider your needs to see if some of them will be eliminated over time. Examples would include loan payments that will amortize debt within a few years and the education funding for your children.

Disability contracts and definitions are complex and vary from company to company, so make sure the person you're dealing with has in-depth knowledge of available product offerings. Where possible, try to get some information about any claims experience for a company before signing on the dotted line. We've heard horror stories from people who've had difficulty trying to collect their benefits when disabled, so be sure to ask the agent:

• Are the benefits integrated with government programs?
• What if I have an unknown pre-existing condition?
• Does the policy have a maximum amount of benefit that can be paid out?

Business Overhead Insurance
Business overhead insurance is tax deductible. While the premiums may seem expensive, there is some comfort in knowing that your government partner in Ottawa is prepared in effect to pay some of the expense. It is therefore prudent to obtain business overhead insurance to cover all of your fixed office expenses and Cash Flow commitments at a minimum. To determine the amount of coverage needed, take the amount of your total expenses (including Cash Flow commitments such as principal prepayment on debt)

and deduct variable expenses. What you have left over should be the amount of coverage you'll need. There are some people who believe that from this amount you should also deduct what your business is producing in the way of revenue that is not dependant on you. You'll have to determine how appropriate this rationale is for your individual business. We have found that in smaller organizations, when the owner is off for an extended period revenue tends to decline even though there can be other employees and producers.

Some office overhead insurance programs offer a declining coverage option. This means that, as time goes on, they pay lower and lower percentages of your costs. For example, after ninety days, benefits are reduced to 75% and so on. The lower premium cost with this type of insurance product can be quite appealing. In talking to business owners who have this type of coverage, the rationale invariably involves the idea of laying off staff. After all, if you're not working, what will the staff do anyway? We recommend that you opt for the type of coverage that covers all of your fixed costs for at least one year or eighteen months. Most entrepreneurs, in our experience, want to go back to their own businesses after a period of disability. While you're off, it's the staff's job to maintain, as much as possible, the goodwill of your customer base. Also, when you go back to work after a disability, it's a great benefit to have trained staff familiar with your operation to support you. Trying to hire and train new people can be frustrating at the best of times; you'll have enough challenges returning to the office after a disability without having to worry about that as well.

Key Person Insurance

Do you have someone in your business who makes a critical contribution? Someone who would be very difficult to replace? If so, you might want to investigate getting some low-cost term insurance on their life. This type of insurance is usually referred to as key person or key employee coverage. It's intended to protect the business against the negative financial impact of the premature death of a highly valued employee who's integral to your success. Some business owners also insure such key employees for disability, but this is much more expensive.

Critical Illness Insurance

This is a relatively new insurance product with coverage similar in many ways to disability insurance. It's often employed in combination with disability coverage. Critical illness insurance could offer valuable coverage in the following situations:

- Providing cash to seek the best and most immediate treatment anywhere in the world.
- Making an injection of cash available in case money must be spent on modifying your house, business environment, and/or car to accommodate your affliction.
- Paying off debt, particularly if you can't get enough disability coverage because of income limitations.
- Supplementing your cash resources to make your last days more comfortable
- If you don't qualify for sufficient disability insurance for a reason that isn't medical, such as your earned income is not high enough.
- Critical illness insurance can also be useful in a case of permanent disability where your insurance benefits would end by age sixty-five and you don't have the investment assets that will grow to provide for you after that point.
- Critical illness insurance can be very expensive and it doesn't cover all illnesses, so be sure you understand what it does cover. A decision to buy this type of cover-

age is one you'll have to make, ideally with the help of your advisory team after a careful analysis of the policy and your needs.

Long-Term Care Insurance (LTCI)

LTCI is relatively new in Canada. It's intended to provide funding for care when you can no longer perform the usual activities of daily living. This is expensive coverage. Terms and definitions also vary from company to company. If you're considering such a policy, examine how they define "usual activities of daily living." Is it the insurance company who decides that you're eligible for such services or is it some independent, unbiased third party? Also, in assessing whether or not you need this coverage, look at what it would cost today if you had to pay for the services covered under the contract directly.

A client who retired recently has more than sufficient capital to provide for an after-tax annual income, that is indexed, equal to what $120,000 would buy in today's dollars. In addition, he has a home and a cottage that are worth a significant amount of money and he is free of debt. He and his wife were considering a long-term care policy. When we looked at what $120,000 after tax would buy today in the way of such services, it became clear immediately that the client and his wife were self-insured. They didn't need to spend the money for this coverage. They could afford to underwrite the risk themselves.

General Insurance

Typically, general insurance includes your home, automobile, and practice. It could also include assets such as a boat or private aircraft. A detailed examination of each of these types of policies is beyond the scope of this book. However, let us emphasize that you should review this coverage regularly. When we're reviewing the affairs of a new client, it's not uncommon to find that their coverage is out of date.

Here are some questions you'll need to answer to guide your review of the policies:

- Who is the insured?
- What is the specific description of the asset or property that is insured?
- Are the amounts of coverage still appropriate?
- What risks are covered and are they appropriate in your circumstances?
- Are there any exclusions?
- Are the deductibles high enough? Keep in mind the rule about only insuring risks you can't afford to insure yourself. A good example of this is comprehensive insurance for your car. Many people pay extra money for a deductible that is quite low, $50 or $100, for example. Most of us can afford a loss of this sum.
- Are there any co-insurance provisions? If you carry less coverage than the co-insurance requirement, a penalty might apply.

Umbrella Coverage

Umbrella insurance is a form of liability insurance that fundamentally stands behind most of your other liability policies (except malpractice or errors-and-omissions coverage). Anyone can fall into a situation where, for whatever reason, they face a significant liability. This insurance is inexpensive and, in our view, the peace of mind it brings makes the expenditure worth it. We once had a client sued for $5,000,000 because of an accident. His liability coverage only went up to $1,000,000. The good news is that after many years, the claim was finally settled for well under $1,000,000, so he was covered. But still, he and his family lived through years of stress and uncertainty that could have been eliminated had he had umbrella coverage.

Errors-and-Omissions Insurance or Malpractice Insurance

We live in an increasingly litigious world, so it is best to protect yourself. If you are able to get this type of insurance for you and your business, buy as much additional coverage as you possibly can, within reason, of course.

Business Contingency Plans

This applies primarily to people who are in smaller organizations. Typically, corporations or partnerships (and some cost-sharing arrangements as well) where you have the benefit of being associated with others on whom you can depend to keep things operating in your absence, have (or should have) agreements that provide for the business' continuity should a member of the group either die or become disabled to the point where they can't return to work.

If you're a solo business person, contingency planning of this nature is important. Ask yourself what would happen to your business if you were to die prematurely or were disabled. The business very often forms a large part of an entrepreneur's family's Net Worth. Goodwill is a perishable item. In the event of premature death, it's difficult enough for your grieving family without having to worry about quickly disposing of your business. All the goodwill you've worked so hard to build up could be lost. Should you become disabled, it could be some time before you know whether or not you'll be able to return to work. In the meantime, who's going to maintain your customer service and goodwill?

A contingency plan might consist of a simple set of policies and procedures within your office, or it could be a more elaborate program. For example, in some professions and service industries it could involve other solo operators in your area with whom you are *comfortable* and willing to associate to deal with this common problem.

If you set up a simple plan within your office, we recommend that you involve your staff in drafting the policies and procedures. After all, they are the ones who have to carry out the plan should something unexpected happen to you. The procedures would include instructions on what to do if you are not available because of some calamity and whom to contact for help (lawyers, accountants, and perhaps key suppliers, etc.). This information should be kept up to date in your policy manual at the office.

If possible, think about having the business valued by a credible business valuator who either sells such commercial enterprises or has contacts who would, and have that valuation kept up to date. If the business needs to be sold in a hurry, the existing valuation will be invaluable. If you can find a business valuator and broker who have expertise in your industry or profession, ask if they have programs whereby after the initial valuation, they update it every year for a nominal sum. Staff are generally in favour of this type of planning because it helps to assure them that they'll continue to have a job should some calamity affect the principal where they're employed.

A self-protection group is another alternative in contingency planning for professional practices and some service industries. Solo practitioners all face similar problems in this area, so it's a good idea to establish an arrangement whereby everyone's practice is protected. While groups vary in size, a minimum of five practitioners is needed. Should one of the group either die or become disabled, there would be four practitioners left who could adjust their schedule so they could spend one day per week in the affected party's office.

In the case of death, there are a couple of ways to plan for this contingency in a self-protection group:
Option One: Have the surviving practitioners maintain the practice to facilitate the sale.

Option Two: Have the surviving practitioners buy the practice. Typically, insurance is put in place for the needed funding. This provides the deceased's family with ready cash and leaves the survivors free to dispose of the practice as they see fit, without the time constraints.

On the disability of one of the members of the group, the other parties would once again adjust their schedules so that they were able to maintain the disabled member's practice; there's usually a time limit established, such as one year. At that point, it's expected that the disabled member would either return to work or the practice would be sold.

In all cases where members of the group are required to adjust their schedules to spend time at another party's practice, fair compensation should be paid. This could be an associate fee agreed upon when the group is set up, a per diem, or some other form of fair compensation. Each party will need to feel comfortable that they can trust the others to act in their best interests and not solicit either staff, clients, or patients.

Starting a Group

If you're interested in starting such a group, begin by getting together with colleagues you trust and with whom you share common practice philosophies. Provided everyone is in agreement, you should document your understanding in a legal agreement. We're not suggesting an agreement for the purposes of enforcement: rather, it should be considered a communication document. It could be in place for a long time before it's needed (ideally, it will never be needed). Having a well-defined agreement allows members to remind themselves of the terms agreed upon.

Written (and Signed) Agreements

Far too many businesses don't have good written agreements in place to properly define the complex relationships within their enterprises. Incidentally, you'll notice in the heading the words in brackets: "and signed." This is another problem with agreements. Several times each year, we have the experience of working with an organization where, on reviewing their arrangements, we find that the principals haven't signed their agreements. They went to the trouble of having them drawn up by a lawyer. They even refer to them from time to time—but they're not signed!

It's critical that you have well thought out agreements in place! This is particularly true if and when you're contemplating a transition. When entrepreneurs don't have such important documentation in place, it's usually because:

- They're very trusting and still believe in the concept of a "handshake agreement,"
- They're concerned about the potential legal expense,
- They don't understand the complexities and try to do it themselves,
- They find the negotiation process preceding an agreement uncomfortable,
- There are other priorities so they just never get around to it, and/or
- The parties know each other and consider themselves friends

Depending on your circumstances, you might need one or more shareholders agreements, partnership agreements, cost-sharing agreements, employment or associate agreements, and so on. No matter which is appropriate in your circumstances, such agreements are best viewed as communication documents when both designing and negotiating them. Most people think that the primary purpose of an agreement is to have something to fall back on in the event of a dispute. While this might be true, we'd like to suggest that one of the most important purposes of a well thought out agreement is to help prevent such disputes.

Over the years of working with entrepreneurs and helping them facilitate their agreements, we've found overwhelmingly that the parties want to be *fair* to each other. What do we mean by *fair*? Here we arrive at the crux of the problem. Interpretation as to what is or isn't fair varies from individual to individual. Generally, most business relationships don't fail because of dishonesty. If someone is dishonest, they'll find a way to "disappoint" you whether there's an agreement in place or not.

The underlying reason business relationships of people who started the arrangement in "good faith" typically fail is because one or more of the parties had unmet expectations. This is why we recommend that you focus on the communication aspects of agreements. Having an in-depth discussion about the important issues prior to entering into a relationship helps the parties reach acceptable compromises in advance. If during this process you find that you can't agree, then be positive. Congratulate yourself. The system worked. It's so much better to find out that you're not compatible before entering into a relationship. You'll save money and you'll avoid all the stress and frustration of either living with an uncomfortable situation or breaking up. Having seen the effects of bad business-relationship breakups, we can't stress enough the importance of this process.

There's another reason to think of good agreements as communication documents: they tend to be in place for a long time. Over time, as everyone knows, memory fades and interpretation can become distorted. If dealing with a contentious issue in the future, you'll always have the ability to refer back to your original understanding. Knowing you can always take the agreement out of the file, blow off the dust, and see clearly what all parties intended, gives you a method of dealing with disagreements before they become serious disputes.

McNulty's Coaching Advice

Have a lawyer translate what you and your colleagues have agreed to into a functional set of legal agreements. When it comes to drafting agreements, try to deal with someone who is familiar with your industry or profession. Don't just accept the agreement that the lawyer proposes. Read it to make sure it expresses what you want. Each party to an agreement should have their own legal representation. Finally, if there's anything you don't understand, question it.

Wills and Powers of Attorney

We can't recall ever meeting a successful business person or professional who didn't understand that they needed a will or a power of attorney. Unfortunately, they didn't always have them in place or keep them current. Once you do get them in place, make sure that your wills and powers of attorney are reviewed regularly and are always up to date. From a risk management perspective, this is as basic as dentists telling their patients to brush regularly.

There's a lot about risk management that can be described as basic common sense. It's about recognizing that we don't always have control over the circumstances that befall us. But we do have control over how we handle them and, more important, how we prepare for them. With a little forethought, you can secure your potential for financial security and success against a variety of contingencies.

Summary

After reading through the material in this book, you now have a comprehensive overview of the financial aspects involved in a successful succession or transition from independent business person to independent retiree. Our hope is that this book becomes a valuable resource for you to turn to throughout your transition process. You'll no doubt find it helpful to re-read specific chapters or sections before making key decisions.

Now that you know about the process involved in planning your transition, there's one important thing you need to make it happen: attitude with a capital "A"! A positive "can do" attitude is essential when you approach the topic of your transition. We know from our experience as wealth managers working with independent business owners and professionals, that many of them at first feel discouraged about money management and their transition prospects in general. Questions we often hear include:

- Where is the money for retirement savings supposed to come from?
- How can people plan the future when it's difficult enough to control the present?
- How much money will I need anyway?
- Will my RRSPs be enough?
- With my busy schedule, where can I find the time to plan and manage a successful transition?
- When should I start preparing for transition?

Unfortunately, there's no end to questions of this nature, and if you aren't able to answer them, it can be very discouraging. We understand your concerns, and it's from this understanding that we say that given time and com-

212 — Barry and Mark McNulty

mitment, you can take control and plan for a positive transition. That's why we wrote this book. It's not just about ideas, methods, and processes that we've seen work over the years, it's also about communicating that the right transition for you is within your grasp. You don't have to be one of those people who has to shrug things off and say your plan is "Freedom 75." It's truly all under your control!

The Power of Positive Thinking

Much has been written about the power of positive thinking. You've probably heard about the importance of having a vision from superior athletes and successful corporations. Vision, by its nature, includes a positive outlook that the goal of either the individual or the group can be accomplished.

You wouldn't be in business if you didn't have the ability to think positively. Your idea to start and build your own enterprise would never have gotten off the ground if you were a negative thinker. In all likelihood, you had a vision and the courage to follow it. Congratulations! Now as you begin to plan for your succession and transition, you'll need to formulate a new vision. Unfortunately, there's not a lot of material or guidance to help you. In truth, it's no wonder there's so much confusion and uncertainty surrounding succession issues. Whether you have an MBA or you're a graduate from the school of hard knocks, most entrepreneurs have little or no training to guide them through the many business and financial activities that will allow them to crown their careers with a successful transition.

We have had the pleasure of working with independent professionals and business owners for a combined total of twenty-five years. This book is a culmination of that experience. It's not a theoretical treatise. Rather, it's tried and true formulas and processes that are based on what we've seen work time and time again. Taking a proactive approach to your transition planning works. No matter what your circumstances, you'll always be better off, barring unforeseen calamities, taking the lead in your transition as outlined and encouraged in this book. We can't communicate this strongly enough. It's possible for almost every entrepreneur and professional to plan for a relatively successful transition if they choose to do so. In fact, it's not only possible but it's your best hope for controlling the outcome.

McNulty's Coaching Advice

Develop a "positive financial attitude" (PFA).

With a PFA and the processes described in this book, it's possible for you to plan a successful transition. Just remember: successful transitions happen by design, not default.

Let us take a moment to quickly recap the key processes covered in this book:

1. Put in place a transition advisory team.

Depending on your individual needs, knowledge base, time, etc., your team should consist of an accountant, lawyer, qualified financial planner and/or investment advisor (if they aren't one and the same), practice valuator, practice broker, perhaps a life planner, and any others you feel could be helpful. Remember, you can't do it all yourself. Even if you have the time, it's unlikely you will have the necessary specialized training and experience. Some of the members of your team will be more active at certain times than others. It will be your job to make sure that they share information when it's required, as well as act in a coordinated manner and keep focused on your needs and objectives.

2. Establish well-defined, reasonable goals.

Have a member of your advisory team quantify them in financial terms so that they can be used as beacons to guide your journey towards transition. Be sure you understand and agree with the assumptions being used in these calculations.

3. Determine as accurately as possible where you are today in a financial sense.

We call this establishing your Current Position. It's your starting point for transition planning, and the financial members of your team should be involved at this time. You might want to re-read chapters two and three to make sure you understand how to instruct these members of your advisory team and what to expect from them.

4. Work with your transition advisory team to establish appropriate strategies.

There are four strategy chapters in this book. The first introduces the topic and helps you determine which of the following three chapters apply to you. Depending on your Current Position, one of these three remaining chapters on strategy should be appropriate for your circumstances. These strategies include making sure you're taking advantage of appropriate tax planning opportunities, some of which are discussed in this book. As well, your plan might include investment strategies—what we like to think of as your pension plan—which are designed to maintain the integrity of your capital, and these can be reviewed again in chapter nine.

5. Make sure your risk management is in order.

6. Monitor your progress and update your plan at least once annually.

Long-term plans are like firing a shot gun. The further

out you go, the less accurate you are. There are two important reasons to monitor your plan. The first has to do with your investment strategies. Regular rebalancing, as mentioned in chapter nine, is a critical component of the overall process. You can't rebalance properly if you don't monitor performance.

The second reason for monitoring is so you can verify that your strategies are working properly and, if necessary, make timely adustments to your plan. The time to find out that your plan didn't work is not a year later when you can't do anything about it.

With respect to annual updates, they allow you to incorporate your past performance; take into account personal, economic, and regulatory changes; and factor in your needs and expectations for the coming year. It's like creating a new starting point every year that will act as a foundation for your strategies for the next twelve months. Through monitoring and updates, you will always be making the appropriate adjustments, which will help you achieve your long-term objectives.

There's So Much Good News on the Horizon

People are living longer now than ever before and we also have an expectation of being healthy for a longer period than in previous generations. A recent study conducted by the Canadian Institute of Actuaries estimates that baby boomers who reach the age of sixty-five in reasonable health have a 50% chance of living to their mid-eighties. Hallmark estimates that in a recent year they sold over eighty thousand 100th-birthday cards. That's incredible. At the same time, there's a hidden message here; you could be retired longer than you worked. If you're going to enjoy a financially comfortable retirement, your chances will be vastly improved by proactive transition planning. Procrastination is a major roadblock when it comes to transition planning but you simply must take action. You can read all the books, listen to as many lectures as you can, and/or get additional training if you want. At the end of the day, it will all be wasted if you don't take action. It's up to you!

When Is the Best Time to Start Planning Your Transition?

The answer to that is easy: when you first graduated from school or first started your business. Now to be candid, no one in our experience has this kind of foresight. *We* certainly didn't. So consider this next question: when is the next best time to start planning your transition? Once again, this question is easy to answer. It's now!

Best of luck on your journey to a successful succession and transition, and beyond!

Glossary of Terms

Adjusted Cost Base (ACB): The cost of an asset that represents what you paid for it and any costs you incurred to improve it. Typically, the ACB is used in the calculation of a capital gain (or loss) upon sale or disposal.

Actuary: A professional who performs the analysis and computation of risks of mortality and morbidity in population groups in order to contribute to establishing appropriate premiums and reserves for insurance companies.

Amortization Period: The time it takes to pay off a debt such as a mortgage, loan, or lease.

Annuity: A contract whereby the owner, referred to as the annuitant, is paid regular payments over a specified period of time, commonly the annuitant's whole life. Unless otherwise specified, the annuity payments end on the annuitant's demise. Annuity contracts can offer a number of variations on terms. For example, such a contract might contain provisions for a minimum period whereby payments are paid to the annuitant, such as ten years. Other variations might provide for the annuity to be indexed, to provide payments to the annuitant's survivor, and so on.

Arms-Length: When two unrelated parties transact business together where each is presumed to be acting in his or her own best interest. It's generally assumed that arms-length arrangements remove concerns about conflicts of interest.

Asset Allocation: How various assets within an investment portfolio are categorized to optimize return and minimize risk.

Attribution: The process of attributing income back to the original taxpayer that results from an ill-conceived strategy to have it taxed in the hands of a lower non-arms-length person in a lower tax bracket.

Audit: A detailed review of an individual's or corporation's financial records and financial documentation for the purpose of certifying the information (financial statement) as correct, or in the case of a government audit, to uncover any circumstances that vary from the government's interpretations and requirements.

Average Tax Rate: Canada has a progressive tax rate system where increasing rates of tax apply to incremental income amounts. Depending on your income, the same rate of tax would not apply to the lower portion of your income as is applied to the highest. As well, before calculating the taxes owing on your income, tax credits, such as your personal tax credit, the equivalent to marriage exemption, and so on, apply. Further deductions such as RRSP contributions reduce your tax. The average rate you pay, therefore, is lower than the top marginal rate. The formula for calculating the average rate is total income, divided into tax paid, equals the average tax rate.

Back-End Load: This is sometimes called a deferred sales charge and it generally refers to commissions and other charges that apply when mutual funds and some life insurance contracts are sold. If the investor or policy holder were to cash in or cancel the contractual arrangement, these charges would be applied first before the return of any of the investor's money. Such redemption charges decline over time to zero.

Basis Point: A term used to break percentage points into hundreds. For example, 1% equals 100 basis points.

Benchmark: An index used in the investment world for performance comparison, such as the Dow Jones Industrial Average, the Standard and Poor's (S&P) 500, or the Toronto Stock Exchange (TSX).

Bear Market: The way a market such as the Toronto Stock Exchange (TSX) is referred to when it's in decline.

Bearish Investment Outlook: An opinion an individual holds that a particular market or markets in general will decline in value.

Bond: A long-term financial debt instrument issued by governments and corporations to raise money from investors in return for the issuer promising to repay on specified terms at a specified interest rate.

Beneficiary: An individual who receives or is entitled to receive the benefit from an insurance policy, RRSP, trust or legal document such as a will.

Benefit Period: Typically applying to disability and business overhead insurance contracts. It defines the maximum period that a benefit will be paid in the event of a claim.

Bond Ladder: Bonds are subject to interest rate risk. A bond ladder that varies maturity rates can help to mitigate this risk. If each year a portion of the portfolio matures and is reinvested at then current rates, the portfolio will always be adjusting to current conditions.

Book Value: The value of an asset as noted in the balance sheet of the company's financial statements.

Bottom Line: A term that refers to the final entry on a Profit and Loss Statement, which is the net profit.

Bottom-Up Business Plan: A business plan that integrates quantified personal objectives, expenses, and tax with one's business including tax and expenses to determine how much revenue or sales volume is required. This format is based on what we refer to as the Golden Rule of Business Planning (either the business earns sufficient income to meet all of your needs including your lifestyle and quantified objectives or you adapt your lifestyle and quantified objectives so that they can be met by what the business produces in income).

Broker: An agent who facilitates the purchases and sales of various financial instruments such as stocks and bonds, usually for a commission.

Bull Market: A market that has been appreciating in value.

Bullish Investment Outlook: The exact opposite of a bearish opinion on the future of a market. In this case, the opinion is that the particular market will increase in value.

Buy/Sell Provisions: The terms in a shareholders, partnership, or cost-sharing agreement that deal with the purchase and sale of the interest of the signatories. Buy/sell provisions typically set out the wishes of what the parties decide in advance relating to premature death, retirement, disability, and a voluntary disposition. It's also common for buy/sell provisions that deal with premature death to require that the parties maintain life insurance to fund the survivors' purchase of the deceased parties' interest. The agreements can also include formulas for deciding on the price and process of buy-outs not triggered by premature death.

Canada Revenue Agency (CRA): The federal tax department.

Canada Depository Insurance Corporation: The Crown corporation that insures bank accounts for banks, trust companies, and credit unions up to a maximum of $60,000 from loss due to a failure of the financial institution.

Canada Pension Plan (CPP): A mandatory government pension plan in all provinces except Quebec (which has the Quebec Pension Plan) that requires the contribution from all people between the ages of eighteen and seventy who earn income from employment.

Canadian Investor Protection Fund (CIPF): A program set up by the Investment Dealers Association and Canadian stock exchanges to protect investors, within limits, from losses resulting from the failure of a member firm.

Canadian Securities Course: An entry-level correspondence course on investing offered by the Canadian Securities Institute. It's a requirement for licensing as a financial advisor/broker for anyone who works for a brokerage firm that's a member of the Investment Dealers Association.

Capital Cost Allowance (CCA): The amount that's deductible from an expense to allow for the impact of wear and tear on the value of your tangible assets. The acquisition value of each asset is added to a pool of assets that fall into a defined CCA class within the Income Tax Act (ITA). When an asset in that pool is disposed of, the amount is applied to reduce the sum of the pool. Each class will have a different capital cost allowance percentage that can be applied to that pool. From a Cash Flow planning perspective, CCA is a non-cash expense, meaning it does not come out of your current available cash.

Capital Dividend Account: Fundamentally, into this account goes the non-taxable portion of capital gains earned by a corporation (see *Capital Gain*) and the proceeds of life insurance benefits paid to the corporation. Such funds can be paid to shareholders in the right circumstances, free of tax, as a capital dividend.

Capital Gain: The profit made when an asset is sold for a price higher than its adjusted cost base. In Canada, only 50% of such capital gains are taxable.

Capital Loss: The loss realized when an asset is sold for less than its adjusted cost base. In Canada, such losses can only be deducted against capital gains. It can be carried back three years or forward seven years to be applied to a capital gain.

Capital Gains Exemption: An exemption available on the sale of shares of a qualified small business corporation or a farm property according to the appropriate terms and regulations of the Income Tax Act (ITA). The exemption applies to a life amount of $500,000 provided all other conditions are met at the time.

Capitalization Rate: A rate used to establish the value of an asset or business. It's calculated by dividing the rate of return someone requires to compensate themselves for the risk and their required profit in making an investment into the normalized profit or Cash Flow of the asset they're interested in acquiring. A simple example would be a person interested in getting an 8% return on an investment they've analyzed and decided to acquire. If the investment is returning $8,000 per year, they would divide this figure by 8% to arrive at the price they would be willing to pay, which is $100,000.

Cash Flow: All income you receive less all expenditures you make. Think of it as "what comes in and what goes out" in monetary terms.

Cash Surrender Value (CSV): The cash amount you would receive from cancelling a permanent life insurance contract such as universal life or whole life, less all surrender charges.

Caveat Emptor: Buyer beware.

Certified Financial Planner (CFP): A designation awarded by the Financial Planning Standards Council of Canada to qualified recipients who have passed a challenging examination, met educational requirements, and are willing to commit to an established code of ethics and continuing education.

Certified Investment Manager (CIM): A designation conferred by the Canadian Securities Institute in recognition of the recipient having completed advanced training in investing and investment management.

Clawback: A sum that must be returned to the government because taxable income in a given year exceeded the limits of a defined threshold. For example, in 2005, Old Age Security begins to be clawed back once your taxable income reaches a little over $60,000 and is fully clawed back when an individual's earned income equals $98,700 or more.

Common Share: A corporate class of stock that signifies ownership of a share of a company, has voting rights, and an entitlement to a share of any profits or losses of the company. Common stockholders are paid last in the event of liquidation of the company, behind creditors and preferred stockholders.

Consumer Price Index (CPI): An index that measures the cost of living for families based on market pricing of what's known as a basket of goods and services. Included in the basket are items such as food, clothing, energy costs, and so on.

Convertible Term Life Insurance: A term life insurance contract that provides the owner with the option to convert the policy to a permanent form of coverage without evidence of insurability.

Corporation: A form of business organization that's separate under the law. Typically, shareholders are protected from liability or loss for other than what they have invested. Professional corporations don't generally protect their owners from professional liability.

Correlation: The method of measuring the relationship between two or more investment assets. A correlation of "plus one" indicates the assets have historically performed exactly the same. Conversely, a correlation of "minus one" would mean that those assets had performed historically in precisely opposite ways.

Criss-Cross Insurance: A term in a shareholders, partnership, or cost-sharing agreement where each of the parties to the agreement maintain life insurance on the other(s) to fund a buyout on death of the deceased signatory's interest.

Current Position: A holistic overview of a person or family's financial circumstances at a particular point in time, which for business owners is integrated with their commercial enterprise(s).

Debenture: An unsecured debt instrument used by corporations as a means of raising funds based on their credit and reputation.

Debt-to-Equity Ratio: A method of measuring the debt level of an individual or company that breaks the amounts involved down to more comparable forms. To arrive at a debt-to-equity ratio, divide liabilities by Net Worth in the case of an individual or debt by shareholders'/partners'/proprietors' equity in the case of a commercial enterprise.

Deemed Disposition: An assumption that all assets are sold, for example on death, to identify taxable capital gains.

Deferred Sales Charge: See *Back-End Load*.

Defined Benefit Pension Plan: A form of employer-sponsored pension plan where, under a formula related to salary and years of service, the pension benefit, the amount the pensioner will receive, is predetermined. It might also include other terms such as indexing for inflation.

Demographics: The study of characteristics and trends in society as indicated by age, sex, occupation, income, family makeup, and so on. The study of demographics has become increasingly important as awareness of the power of the buying habits and political leanings of the so-called baby boomers has become evident. From a transition perspective, there is some debate on what impact baby boomers who own businesses and professional practices will have on the market.

Disability Insurance: Insurance coverage intended to help you pay for your lifestyle and other expenses should you become disabled and unable to work.

Discounted Cash Flow: A form of financial analysis generally used to evaluate a business or investment's anticipated Cash Flows. It can also be used to compare different investment alternatives that have different inflows and outflows of cash.

Discretionary Cash: A term used to describe the portion of your Cash Flow that's uncommitted, as opposed to the portion that must go to paying for food, shelter, debt, and other necessary expenses. Discretionary Cash represents funds where a choice can be made on where to spend the money, such as entertainment, vacations, or buying a new couch.

Diversification: Distributing the risk of investment over a variety of securities. In effect, it's the "don't put all your eggs in one basket" philosophy. Ideally, diversification shouldn't just add different assets at random but rather assets that, through historic performance, can be expected to complement each other and help the investor manage risk.

Dividend: A method of paying out after-tax profits of a corporation to its shareholders. A dividend credit is available on dividends from Canadian corporations to offset the fact that the shareholder's corporation has already paid tax on this income.

EAFE Index: A benchmark prepared by the Morgan Stanley investment group that represents Europe, Australia, and the Far East.

Earned Income: Generally thought of as income from employment such as salary, commissions, or bonus; it also includes real-estate rentals and self-employed income of a proprietor or partner.

Efficient Frontier: A graphical depiction reflecting the risk/reward characteristics of all portfolios with positions ranging from 100% equity to 100% cash.

Equities: Shares of corporations representing the ownership or "equity" in the firm.

Estate: The total sum of all assets owned by a person upon their death.

Estate Freeze: A complicated planning strategy whereby the value of a person's estate is frozen and future growth passed on to the next generation in a tax-efficient manner.

Estate Taxes: There are no estate taxes in Canada per se, other than Probate Taxes. When someone passes away in Canada, there's a deemed disposition of all of their assets for the purposes of determining capital gains. A rollover is available under the Income Tax Act (ITA) whereby ownership of those assets that have a capital gain can be transferred to the deceased's spouse at his or her adjusted cost base (ACB) so that no capital gains must be recognized at least until the surviving spouse passes. Otherwise, if capital gains exist at the time of death and there is no spouse or no election made to roll the asset over, 50% of the capital gains recognized through the deemed disposition will become taxable income for the estate.

Estate Planning: Formalized strategies to reduce tax liability and pass on an individual's wealth to his or her designated heirs in accordance with the individual's wishes.

Excess RRSP Contributions: An amount contributed to an RRSP in excess of their annual regulated limit. RRSP limits are 18% of a person's prior year's earned income, subject to a maximum amount. In 2005, the maximum was $16,500. For 2006, the maximum contribution amount is expected to be $18,000; in 2007, $19,000; in 2008, $20,000; in 2009, $21,000; in 2010, $22,000; and thereafter, it is to be indexed.

Exchange Traded Funds (ETFs): A trust listed on a stock exchange that represents an index.

Face Value: The amount of coverage of a life insurance contract or the issue amount of a bond or other similar security.

Fair Market Value (FMV): A notional opinion of value for a business or other asset that a qualified valuator estimates a willing seller and a willing buyer in possession of all the facts, without any compulsion to act, would consummate a sale for expressed in dollar terms. It's considered notional because no actual sale takes place.

Family Trust: Officially referred to as an inter vivos trust, it's an arrangement sanctioned under the Income Tax Act (ITA) that permits assets to be held and administered for the benefit of the beneficiaries. Family Trusts are popular vehicles to use for income-splitting strategies with other family members, particularly one's children, nieces, and nephews. One of the key benefits is that the assets remain in the control of the trustees of the trust.

Financial Advisor: A person who advises clients on the purchase or sale of investment or insurance products, usually on a commission basis. An increasing number of financial advisors are now working, or at least offering their services, on a fee-for-service basis.

Financial Independence: A relative term used to describe the financial position of a person or family that has achieved the ability, through the buildup of sufficient wealth, to be self-supporting without working. This means that they're in a position to work out of choice rather than necessity. This is an objective that many business owners, including independent professionals, identify as a priority as opposed to establishing a firm transition date. For example, you might set a goal at age forty-five to be financially independent at age sixty. You are then free to decide when and how you'll complete your transition.

Financial Planning Standards Council (FPSC): A non-profit professional organization that establishes ethical practices; standards of education including continuing education requirements; and awards the Certified Financial Planner designation to individuals who've met their mandated criteria.

Fiscal Year: The financial year of a business, whether incorporated or not. Unlike individuals, who in Canada have a year-end of December 31st, the fiscal year of a business can be a non-calendar year.

Fixed Expenses: Business or personal costs to which you're committed, regardless of variables such as activity or revenue.

Fixed Income: A general term used to categorize interest-bearing investments with a maturity at the time of issue in excess of one year.

Front-End Load: A method of charging commissions at the time of the initial purchase of an investment, usually mutual funds.

Generally Accepted Accounting Principles (GAAP): A system of rules and procedures that define Canadian accounting practices.

General Partnership: There are two types of partnerships: general and limited. Under a general partnership, all parties are free to take an active role in the day-to-day affairs of the business. Also, general partners have joint and several liability with the other partners. Typically, partnership agreements specify that each of the partners is indemnified from a liability of one individual partner that has nothing to do with the business or for which the individual did not have the authority to commit the other partners.

Goodwill: An intangible asset that expresses the value of future earnings of a business. Professional goodwill relates to the goodwill that the business has because of the owner. This is typically seen in a smaller enterprise largely dependent on its success because of the skills and/or reputation of one individual. It has no value because it can't be passed on. Commercially transferable goodwill, on the other hand, has value. It represents such things as branding, location, and processes that a purchaser can reasonably expect will accrue to a new owner.

Guaranteed Investment Certificate (GIC): A form of deposit, usually non-cancellable for a fixed term, offered by a bank, trust company, or other financial institution, that's guaranteed by the deposit-taking entity to pay a specified interest rate and a return of deposit.

Income Capitalization: One of a number of methods of valuing real estate or a business investment. The formula is income divided by the required rate of return.

Income Trust: A commercial enterprise structured so that revenue from income-producing assets, after deducting expenses and retaining sufficient funds for working capital and anticipated expenditures, is directly distributed to the trust holders.

Index: An indicator reflecting the value of the assets of which it's made up—the S&P/TSX, the Dow Jones Industrial Average (DJIA), or Standard & Poor's 500 index (S&P 500), for example. Such indexes act as benchmarks that can provide an indication of the direction of the appropriate market it's intended to represent. Indexes provide an excellent yardstick for comparison of the performance of certain individual securities relative to the overall market.

Inflation: The most public measure of inflation is the consumer price index, which measures the increase or decrease of a "basket of household items and staples."

Input Tax Credits: A system of reimbursement to businesses for the GST they have paid for goods and/or servic-

232 — Barry and Mark McNulty

es sold to their customers who pay GST on the end-product sale price. The intention is to prevent what can be thought of as double GST taxation.

Intestate: A term used to describe an individual who has died without leaving a valid will.

Inter Vivos Trust: Fundamentally, a more technical term for a family trust. Inter vivos means that the trust is set up in your lifetime as compared to a testamentary trust established on death through your will.

Joint Last to Die: The event upon which a joint life insurance contract will pay the benefit of the policy to the named beneficiary or estate.

Joint Ownership: A form of legal title of an asset such as real estate. Upon the death of one of the joint owners, the title typically passes on to the survivor(s).

Joint and Several Liability: All parties to an agreement that creates liability are responsible either as individuals or jointly. General partnerships are an example of structures where joint and several liabilities exist.

Joint Venture: An enterprise undertaken by two or more parties.

Junk Bond: A speculative bond that generally pays a higher rate of interest to attract investors and compensate them for the additional risk.

Kiddie Tax: Legislation enacted within the last few years that requires taxation at the top marginal rates, without deduction, on any dividend income from a private company paid through a trust (or directly for that matter) or any income from property such as rent that is allocated to beneficiaries under the age of eighteen.

Leverage: Another term for a liability that probably has its roots in the idea of "leveraging" your assets or Net Worth by borrowing against them. While leveraging can effectively increase the investment return on the equity in your assets, it also increases risk.

Life Income Fund: A conversion option that applies to locked-in RRSPs (see below), similar to a registered retirement income fund (RRIF) (see below).

Life Planning: An important part of the transition process that deals with the non-financial aspects of an individual's retirement. It's the plan for how you're going to spend the time, in a satisfying way, that you used to spend at your business. In our experience, unless this is addressed, entrepreneurs and professionals can wind up feeling very bored with retirement and might actually seek out some form of employment—not for the money, but for something to do.

Limited Partnership: There are two types of partnership: general and limited. Under a Limited Partnership, a general partner exists to run the business enterprise and to which all liability of the business accrues. Under a limited partnership, the limited partners are protected against liability beyond the loss of their initial investment (including funds borrowed for that investment) but must take no part in the day-to-day management of the business that is the subject of the partnership.

Locked-In RRSPs: An RRSP that has been established with the transfer to it of pension assets. The capital within the locked-in RRSP cannot be accessed until it has been converted to a life income fund.

Management Expense Ratio (MER): The management fee charged by mutual fund managers to cover the costs of managing your investments including their services, costs of marketing, commissions, and profits. A lot has been written about the negative effects that MERs can have on your investment performance. It might appear that MERs are more expensive compared to doing the management yourself but it takes a lot of time and effort to properly manage your investments, and for most business owners, time is an expensive commodity. An alternate way to evaluate MERs is to consider whether or not you receive value for those expensive fees. We define value in MERs as relative performance that at least meets, but ideally exceeds, an appropriate index. If you find this measure of value reasonable, you might want to compare performance of a fund specializing in U.S. mutual funds with the S&P 500. Sadly, of the thousands of mutual funds available to Canadian investors, only a few consistently measure up to this standard.

Marginal Tax Rate: Canada has a progressive tax rate where the higher your income within defined limits, the higher the tax rate that will apply to the incremental amount.

Market Risk: Also known as systematic risk, market risk refers to the volatility of the whole market. If you own a portfolio that includes Canadian equities listed on the Toronto Stock Exchange and the whole market declines by say 20%, so will that portion of your portfolio. This is one of the many reasons that diversification is important in formulating investment strategies.

Market Timing: The ability or attempt to establish the right time to buy into the market and the right time to get out. Studies have shown that while everyone would like to believe that someone can call such movements in the markets accurately, it's just not possible on a consistent basis. If it were, the person would be fabulously wealthy. Also, why would they tell us the right time to buy or sell? If investors as a whole knew that information, who would there be to buy when this pundit wanted to sell? And who would sell when this person wanted to buy? The concept just doesn't work consistently!

Money Purchase Pension Plan: An employer-sponsored pension program that's the opposite of a defined benefit pension plan. This type of plan grows through contributions and investment returns. When the employee retires, rather than there being a set formula as in a defined plan, the cumulative value is used to purchase whatever retirement benefits this cumulative sum will buy.

Multiple Wills: A strategy that has been developed to reduce probate fees. In effect, two wills are drawn up: one that deals with items that are definitely subject to probate and the other that will not require probate. Make sure you have good legal advice if you are using this strategy. You don't want the second will to invalidate the first.

NASDAQ: A facility owned by the U.S. National Association of Securities Dealers that electronically handles the trading of "over the counter" stocks.

NASDAQ Index: An index that reflects the performance of over-the-counter stocks traded on the NASDAQ.

Net Worth: The difference between a person's or family's assets and their liabilities, in other words, between what they have and what they owe.

Net Worth Statement: Similar to a balance sheet used in business financial statements, a Net Worth Statement is a detailed snapshot of an individual's or family's assets, liabilities, and Net Worth at a particular moment in time.

No-Load Mutual Fund: A mutual fund that doesn't pay either front-end or back-end commissions or trailer fees. Often, such no-load funds have a lower MER and are distributed directly to the public as opposed to being marketed through registered intermediaries.

Non-Competition Agreement: An agreement generally required by the purchaser of a business (be it a corporation, partnership interest, or proprietorship) that restricts the vendor from competing with that business for a specified period of time and, if applicable, in a specified geographic area.

Old Age Security (OAS): A government pension plan that is payable to all Canadians beginning at age sixty-five. To be entitled to the full OAS benefit, a recipient must have been in residence in Canada for a minimum of forty years after the age of eighteen. If a Canadian has been in residence in this country for a minimum of ten years after the age of eighteen, he or she would be entitled to a partial benefit. Once an entitlement to an OAS benefit is established, it will be paid regardless of whether or not the recipient is a resident of Canada. There is a clawback provision whereby benefits start to be clawed back when your taxable income reaches $60,806 (for 2005). The benefit is fully clawed back by the time taxable income reaches $98,700.

Opportunity Cost: Conceptually, the cost of every positive action is the foregone opportunity available in other alternatives not pursued. In a very simplified example, if you have $10,000 and the choice between investing it in the stock market or paying off a debt with an interest rate of 7% per annum and you decide to invest in the stock market, the opportunity cost would be 7%. Your opportunity cost is used in discounted Cash Flow analysis in which you evaluate the characteristics of different investment alternatives by discounting the various anticipated benefits to present values using this rate.

Over-Contribution of RRSP Maximum Limits: One can contribute a maximum of $2,000 in excess of the pre-scribed RRSP contribution limit without incurring a penalty. A contribution in excess of this amount will attract a fine of 1% per month until such a time as the plan is brought into compliance.

Over the Counter (OTC): The term used to describe trading in securities that aren't listed on any accredited exchange, typically because they can't meet one or more of the requirements for listing.

Pension: Traditionally refers to a program established by an employer or government body to provide a qualified retiree with an income stream on which to live when they're no longer employed. In a broader sense, we consider it to be the accumulation of all assets (both registered and non-registered investments) that an individual builds up over their lifetime to provide income once they're retired.

Pension Income Tax Credit: In the year you turn age sixty-five and in subsequent years, you're entitled to a pension income credit, which is the lesser of $1,000 or the amount of your pension. Payments from an RRSP,

238 — Barry and Mark McNulty

annuity, pension, and RRIF (not including OAS or CPP) are considered pension income for the purposes of this tax credit. If you turn sixty-five, have no employer-sponsored pension income, and don't plan to convert your RRSPs until later (up to the year you turn sixty-nine), you might want to consider taking a minimum of $1,000 out of your RRSP as income since there is no carry-forward of this tax credit.

Permanent Life Insurance: Insurance intended to cover you for your entire life, such as universal life insurance or what's known as "whole life."

Personal Living Expenses (PLE): The cumulative sum required to maintain your lifestyle expenses, not including debt service, savings, RRSPs, and unusual non-recurring items such as renovations.

Power of Attorney: An important legal document useful in the risk management of your affairs. It provides someone you trust, typically a spouse, with your authority to act in your stead should something unexpected occur that prevents you from dealing with your affairs or in a situation where you're unavailable to deal with your affairs.

Preferred Shares: A class of stock in a corporation that receives dividends, usually at a specified rate, in preference to dividends paid on common shares and which would receive preference over common shares in the event that the company is dissolved. Preferred shares often, but not always, have no voting rights.

Prescribed Annuity: An annuity purchased with non-registered capital whereby the issuer, usually an insurance company, provides regular payments, generally for life, to the annuitant. The payments receive favourable income tax treatment because they're considered, in part, a return of your capital. In other words, it's a financial product in which Cash Flow is high and taxable income is low, particularly in the initial years of the arrangement. Like all annuities, there are many terms to be considered, such as indexing, minimum guaranteed payment period, and so on.

Present Value Analysis: See *Discounted Cash Flow* and *Opportunity Cost.*

Principal Residence Exemption: In Canada, a capital gain on your principal residence is exempt from taxation. You're only allowed one principal residence per family, which by definition includes children under the age of eighteen.

Probate: The legal process of going through the courts to confirm or appoint the executor(s) of a deceased person's will.

Quebec Pension Plan (QPP): A Quebec government program similar to the Canada Pension Plan (CPP). CPP is not available in Quebec.

Registered Education Savings Plan (RESP): A program established to help Canadians save for educational needs. A maximum of $4,000 per year per child with an overall limit of $42,000 can be contributed to the plan. In addition, the Canada Education Savings Grant (CESG) provides for 20% of the yearly contribution to a maximum of $7,200 per child under the age of eighteen. Depending on the age of your child, you might want to contribute less than the maximum allowable amount each year so as to ensure the plan receives the maximum $7,200 limit for the CESG. While contributions aren't deductible, the assets within the plan grow tax-free. A further advantage is that when the child goes to a qualifying post-secondary institution, the income withdrawn is taxed in his or her hands.

Registered Retirement Income Fund (RRIF): An RRIF is an RRSP conversion option whereby your RRSP assets are transferred into the RRIF by the end of the year you turn sixty-nine. Lump sum payments from a registered pension plan can also be transferred to an RRIF. The assets within the RRIF, like in your RRSP, continue to grow tax-free. However, there are two main differences: you can no longer make contributions to the plan and the plan must pay out a minimum amount of retirement income to you starting no later than the year after you convert to the RRIF. Payments out of the RRIF are fully taxable except that you can defer tax on a withdrawal by rolling it over to a life annuity. While there is a requirement for a minimum payout, there's no maximum restriction. RRIFs can be self-administered and you can have more than one of them.

Registered Retirement Savings Plan (RRSP): A program to allow individuals to set aside savings on a deferred tax basis in order to build reserves for their retirement. Contributions are based on 18% of an individual's previous year's earned income to a prescribed maximum. They are tax deductible and assets within the plan grow tax-free. Be aware that any investment losses can't be replaced within the RRSP. Not only is the money lost, but the negative impact is compounded by the loss of future tax-free growth. We strongly recommend that you use your RRSPs as the place to hold secure and safer investments, which typically earn interest and therefore benefit greatly from the tax-free compounding.

Retirement Compensation Arrangement (RCA): A supplemental retirement planning alternative enshrined in the Income Tax Act (ITA) that is established by an employer for the benefit of an employee. Contributions to the plan by the employer are fully deductible provided they're reasonable in the circumstances. Fifty percent of such contributions must be sent to Canada Revenue Agency (CRA) where the funds are set aside in what's known as a refundable tax account. The other 50% is invested in a trust for the benefit of the employee. When the employee retires, for every $2 drawn from the trust, CRA sends back $1 to the trust. The impact therefore is that the trust went down a net of $1 and the refundable tax account went down by the same amount. It can work well, particularly if the employee is able to bring the funds received from the trust back into income at a lower average rate of tax.

Retiring Allowance: A sum paid by an employer on the retirement of an employee in recognition of long years of service. It is deductible to the employer and, under the special RRSP contribution rules, within prescribed limits, can be placed directly into the employee's RRSP without any source deductions.

Reverse Mortgage: A mortgage on your home in which tax-free funds are made available to you, within limits, for your retirement living needs. Generally, no payments have to be made until you sell. While there are some concerns about this product and the fact that the interest compounds, it can be very useful in keeping your taxable income low enough to avoid the OAS clawback and your Cash Flow high. Careful analysis of the pros and cons should be done before going ahead with such a plan.

S&P/TSX Composite Index (S&P/TSX): An index that tracks the broad performance of the 300 largest stocks on the Toronto Stock Exchange.

Segregated Funds: Similar to mutual funds, these investments are offered by insurance companies. They have a couple of potential advantages as compared to mutual funds. One is that they are considered insurance contracts and can offer creditor protection. The other is that they include a guarantee that you'll get all or a percentage of all your money back if you leave the money invested for a minimum amount of time, commonly ten years. As a word of caution, watch their MERs, they can be quite high.

Shareholders' Agreement: A contract established for the benefit of all shareholders to govern the terms of their relationship. If a shareholders' agreement is not put in place, their relationship will be governed by the applicable jurisdiction's corporate legislation under which the company was incorporated.

Spousal RRSP: As an alternative to making a contribution to their own plan, a taxpayer may make what's known as a spousal contribution to a plan registered in their spouse's name. The amount of the contribution is calculated in the same way a normal RRSP contribution would be determined. The contributor is entitled to the tax deduction, even though the assets are in the spouse's name. Spousal RRSPs can be a good income-splitting vehicle.

Spousal Trust: A testamentary trust established through a will for the benefit of the deceased's spouse. Such trusts are often set up as part of an estate plan. The benefit amounts to income-splitting in that the earnings on assets within the trust are taxed separately from the individual's. Under a spousal trust, only the spouse should be a beneficiary. In a situation where, either through life insurance, existing assets, or a combination of both, a significant amount of money would be left to the spouse, the income from which could be expected to put that spouse well into the top marginal tax bracket, consideration should be given to adding provisions in the will to establish such a trust.

Standard & Poor's 500 Stock Index (S&P 500): A U.S. stock index. (See *Index* above.)

Strip Bond: Bonds, usually issued by the government, that have the interest coupons stripped from the principal. Each is sold separately at a discount that is supposed to reflect a yield that is competitive with current interest rates for similar credit risks with similar maturities.

Tangible Assets: Physical assets such as equipment, real estate, cash, accounts receivable, vehicles, etc.

Tax Shelter: An investment where at least part of the advantage being offered is tax savings, tax deferral, or a combination of both.

Term Life Insurance: A type of life insurance that covers you for a specific period of time. It doesn't include any investment component or the prospect of any cash surrender value buildup. It simply provides family or other designated beneficiaries with a cash payout in the amount of the policy in the case of the insured's premature death.

Testamentary Trust: A trust created upon the death of an individual as stated in their will. Common uses of such a trust are cases where minor children must be provided for or when a spousal trust (see above) is appropriate from an estate-planning perspective.

Time Value of Money: The recognition that a dollar today is worth more than a dollar in the future.

Trailer Fee: An annual fee paid by a mutual fund to the party who originally sold the investment in order to encourage the provision of ongoing advice and service to the investor. The payment of these fees is incorporated in the mutual fund's MER.

Transition (also called Succession): As used in the context of this book, the process of moving from active business ownership through to retirement. There are three phases to transition. In the pre-transition phase, you prepare your business for sale; lay the groundwork for tax strategies to be used in the next two phases; create a "pension" to provide financial security in the third phase; and develop hobbies, support networks, and other non-financial aspects to give your life satisfaction during the third phase. In the transition phase, you deal with the sale of your business; staff, customers, or clients; the legal and tax issues; and many other complexities. In the post-transition phase, you realize your retirement vision and enjoy the rest of your life!

Universal Life Insurance: Insurance that has two main components: a term life insurance contract and an investment component. The term life insurance is usually either yearly renewable term coverage (YRT) or term-to-100 (i.e. age 100) coverage. Where the amount of insurance and the investment components are aligned in accordance with a government formula, the investment component grows free of tax within the policy.

Umbrella Insurance: A type of supplementary liability insurance that stands behind your other liability policies to provide additional coverage. The cost is usually quite reasonable relative to the size of the benefit.

Unsystematic Risk: Where the risk relates to a characteristic of the individual investment as opposed to the whole market. An example of unsystematic risk would be when a stock price declined in value due to a larger than anticipated loss.

Wealth Management: A holistic approach to the management of one's financial affairs, including not only investments but also tax planning, estate planning, risk management, income and cash management, and so on. Generally, this service is provided on a fee-for-service basis and is of interest to individuals who have a relatively high Net Worth.

Whole Life Insurance: A form of permanent life insurance (other than universal life) that provides a combination of insurance coverage and the potential to build cash surrender values. Premiums are level and could be payable for your entire life if the coverage is to remain in force.

Appendix
Chapter One

Chart for organizing goals (Listed in order of priority)

Goal	Description	Who	Deadline

Comments on Some Common Transition Scenarios

1. Full transition – outside purchaser

In this instance, you either exit immediately or continue working for a short period of time to facilitate the transfer of goodwill to the purchaser.

The Pros:
• You get all your money out at one time.
• There are no continued staff or management responsibilities.
• You pass on responsibility for care of your enterprise quickly and efficiently.

The Cons:
• Your change from a full-time business owner is very rapid, with no time to "ease into retirement." While the financial part of the equation might be appropriate, the non-financial aspects of this alternative could prove challenging.
• You lose any entitlement to future business growth and profits.
• If you're in a small community or in a very competitive environment, care should be taken to keep the fact that you're selling confidential until you have a firm purchase agreement.

2. Full transition to a partner

In this case, you get the best results when obtaining an independent third-party valuation. You might also want to hire a facilitator to rough out the basic terms of the transition so that you'll be in a better position to instruct your lawyers and accountants on what you want.

The Pros:
• You get all your money right away.
• Typically, you have a little more control on the timing of your exit.

- You're relieved of staff and management responsibilities.
- The sale can be kept confidential.

The Cons:
- If you've been in business with someone for some time, personal feelings and expectations can cloud some negotiation issues. In addition, some agreements that have been in place for a long time may have had buy/sell provisions that are not appropriate in today's marketplace. For example, we worked with a client who had been in a partnership for over thirty years. When the client's health declined and he wanted to sell, we found that the old agreement stipulated that the buy out price would be based on the value of the tangible assets only. When the agreement had been put in place, goodwill had very little real value. Sadly, his partners did not want to recognize the fact that goodwill does have a value today. They insisted on sticking to the terms of the agreement. In this particular case, the difference was well in excess of $1,000,000.

3. *Partial Transition to an employee or employees – partnership*

In a partnership structure, there can be many formulas for the sharing of profits. In some cases for example, all revenue goes into a "common pot" and after the expenses of doing business are removed, partners simply share in the profits on a proportional basis relative to their partnership interest. In other situations we are familiar with, each partner might receive a proportion of their own production or personal revenue generation, with the balance going into the "common pot" along with the revenue produced by employees who are not partners, and the profits remaining after payment of expenses are shared proportionately. In other cases, the profits are shared on a ratio that relates to each partner's revenue generation. These are only a few common examples. There can be many variations. As the formula should have a direct bearing on the price a new partner pays, it is a very good idea to properly define exactly what the new partner is purchasing.

The Pros:
- You spread your financial risk because your partner(s) is/are there to share the investment, liability, and costs.
- You may have more confidence when away on holidays with your partner 'minding the store'.
- Management duties can be shared with greater confidence.
- Synergy can be enhanced.
- It can be a great way to retain the services of vital employees.
- There is a logical buyer for your partnership interest when you want to do a final transition.

The Cons:
- Since partners typically share everything, you have less flexibility for independent action. For example, you may be required to work a minimum amount or produce a minimum level of personal production.
- Because of the close relationship of the parties, disagreements can be more stressful. Extensive 'Buy/Sell' arrangements should be included in your partnership agreements to protect the value of your partnership interest.
- There can be liability issues to contend with that you should discuss with your legal advisor.

4. Partial transition to an employee or employees – sale of shares of corporation

There are a number of complexities to consider when selling shares of your corporation to an employee. Whether you are selling a minority interest, a controlling interest or some amount in between, the practical similarities are very similar to a partnership. We can think of a corporation with multiple shareholders as simply another form of partnership in a different legal structural format. Having a well thought out shareholders' agreement is very important. It is also important to define revenue and profit-sharing formulas under a corporate structure as well as in a partnership as mentioned above. In the corporation, however, this revenue entitlement is typically defined as salaries, commissions, and bonuses. It can even extend to the frequency or other criteria for the issue of dividends.

The Pros:
- You spread your investment among the other shareholders by, in effect, "partially cashing out."
- There can be greater confidence that someone is "minding the store" when you go on holidays.
- Management duties can be shared more readily. Of course, this is something you will likely be doing anyway in preparation for your final transition.
- Synergy can be enhanced.
- It could be a method of retaining the services of a vital employee.
- There is a logical buyer for the balance of your shares when you want to do a final transition.

The Cons:
- Like a non-incorporated partnership, you have less flexibility for independent action. For example, as the sole owner of a corporation, you might be in a position to employ a family member. We have seen many situations where this can become a problem when another shareholder "buys in."
- With the close relationship of the parties, disagreements can be more stressful. A well thought out shareholders' agreement is absolutely vital.

5. Partial transition – selling a division or portion of your business

Under this form of partial transition, another party, often an employee, purchases a portion of your business which can be completely separated from the whole without negatively affecting the enterprise's viability. This transition variation can work in either a partnership or a corporate environment.

The Pros:
- You benefit from the sale proceeds and all that entails.
- You are still 100% in control of the portion of your business that is not sold. You retain your flexibility for independent action.
- It might be possible to slow down somewhat as your responsibilities are reduced.
- In many such situations, the sale of a portion of your business allows you to focus your energies more directly on the balance that you retain with very positive results.

The Cons:
- Typically, this format does not further your final transition plans.
- You can no longer enjoy the revenue and potential of the division or portion of your business that has been sold off.

6. Merging with a competitor

This concept can work well in situations where the business is not large or perhaps you are a sole practitioner professional who has started to slow down and have reached a point where it's no longer practical to justify your own operation. It's also worth considering if you plan to slow down in the near future. The pros and cons of this concept greatly depend on your objectives and your ability to match up with someone whose objectives are the same as or at least don't conflict with yours. Part of the motivation for both parties should be your eventual full transition. It is important to negotiate in advance the transition terms that will satisfy you, as you could be at a disadvantage after the merger. When you are ready to retire is not the time to be thinking about moving out on your own again in order to get the best price and terms for your business. The logistics are just too difficult. This means that you could well have lost your leverage in any negotiation.

Chapter Two

Unincorporated Business Cash Flow Planning Worksheet

	Last Year-End	Projected Changes	This Year
Gross Revenue			
Less Cost of Goods Sold			
Less General and Admin. Expenses			
Fixed			
Wages			
Rent			
Leases			
Bank Charges			
Interest			
Professional Fees			
Maintenance			
Utilities			
Phone			
Ads and Promotion			
Insurance			
Professional fees			
Prof. Development			
Other			
Variable			
Shipping			
Commissions			
Office Supplies			
Other			
Total Expenses			

	Last Year-End	Projected Changes	This Year
Plus			
Non-Cash Expense			
Personal Credit Card Use			
Increase in Debt			
Accounts Receivable at beginning of year			
Collections for the period			
Minus			
Uncollectables			
Debt Repayment			
Purchases			
Accounts Receivable at end of period			
Total Pre-Tax Funds Available			

Net Personal Inflow & Outflow Summary

Inflow	Amount	Outflow	Amount
You		Income Tax	
Unincorporated Business		Income Tax (spouse)	
Business Net Income		**Total Income Tax**	
Dividends		All Lifestyle Expenditures	
Interest		House Taxes	
Proceeds from Borrowings		Vacations (estimate only)	
		Other	
Spouse		**Total Living Expenses**	
Spouse's Salary		Car Payments	
Spouse's Business Income		Mortgage Payments	
Dividends		Other	
Interest		**Total Debt Service**	
		Savings	
Other Family Members		RRSP Contribution	
Salaries to Children		RRSP Contribution (spouse)	
Dividends to Children		Other	
over Eighteen		**Total Savings**	
Totals		**Total Outflow**	
		Deficit/Surplus	

Chapter Three

Section One: Personal Net Worth Statement

As of _____	Name	Name	Corporations	Total
Assets				
Short Term Liquid Assets				
Cash in Personal Bank Accounts				
Cash in Business Accounts				
Money Market Funds				
T-Bills				
Total Liquid				
Business Market Value				
Accounts Receivable				
Other				
Other				
Other				
Total Business				

As of _____

	Name	Name	Corporations	Total
Registered Investment Assets				
RRSPs				
Pension (if any)				
RCAs				
Total Registered				
Non-Registered Investment Assets				
Cash				
Stocks/Mutual Funds				
Bonds/GICs				
Real Estate				
CSV of Life Insurance				
Other				
Other				
Total Investments				
Children's Investments				
RESP				
In Trust For Funds				

As of ___	Name	Name	Name	Corporations	Total
Other					
Other					
Total Children's Investments					
Personal-Use Assets					
House					
Cottage					
Cars					
Art					
Jewelry					
Boats/trailers					
Other					
Other					
Total Personal					
Total Assets					

Section Two: Personal Net Worth Statement

As Of _____	Name	Name	Total	%
Liabilities				
Short-Term N.D. Personal*				
Loans Due this year				
Credit Cards				
Lines of Credit				
Tax Arrears				
Other				
Total Short-Term Personal				
Long-Term N.D. Personal*				
House Mortgage				
Cottage Mortgage				
Car Loans				
Insurance Policy Loans				
Other				
Total Long-Term Personal				

As Of	Name	Name	Total	%
Investment Debt				
Stocks/Mutual Funds				
Real Estate				
Tax Shelters				
Total Inv Debt				
Unincorporated Business Debt				
Bank Line of Credit				
Accounts Payable				
Building Mortgages				
Long-Term Loans				
Leases				
Total Business Debt				
Total Liabilities				

As Of _____	Name	Name	Total	%
Net Worth				
Total Assets	____	____	____	____
Less				
Total Liabilities	____	____	____	____
Total Net Worth	____	____	____	____
Transition Net Worth	____	____	____	____

*N.D. means interest cost is non-deductible for tax purposes

Chapter Six

Bottom-Up Business Plan: Proprietorship

Annual Required Revenue /
days (weeks or months) worked in the year _____

(A) All Business Operating Costs _____
(B) Non-Cash Expenses
  (CCA, Depreciation) _____
(C) Business Capital Expenditures
    required this year _____

Annual Gross Required Revenue (A+B+C+K) _____

(D) Projected Income Tax _____
(E) PLE (Personal Living Expense) _____
(F) Periodic Expense
    (Car, renovations, repairs, etc) _____
(G) Personal Debt Service _____
(H Business Debt Principal Payments _____
(I) RRSPs _____
(J) Annual Cost of Quantified Goals _____

K=Required Pre-Tax Profit and
  Non-Cash Expense (D+E+F+G+H+I+J) _____

Bottom-Up Business Plan: Incorporated Business

Daily (weekly, monthly) Required Revenue _____

Annual Required Revenue / days

   (weeks or months) worked in the year _____

(A) = Annual Gross Required Revenue _____

(B) Management Salary to Owner _____

(C) **plus** All Other Business Expenses _____

(D) **plus** Non-Cash Expense _____

(E) **plus** Principal Repayment on Debt _____

(F) Corporate Pre-Tax Profit _____

(G) **minus** Corporate Tax _____

(H) Corporate A/T Profit available _____

(I) Required corporate A/T profit for savings in
corporations, dividend income to shareholders
based on planned salary/dividend mix and any
required corporate working capital _____

Personal

(J) Personal Income Tax _____

(K) PLE (Personal Living Expense) _____

(L) Periodic Expense

   (Car, renovations, repairs, etc.) _____

(M) Personal Debt Service _____

(N) RRSPs _____

(O) Planned Goal Savings in Corporation _____

(P) Annual Cost of Quantified Goals _____

Required Income (Salary and Dividends)

   from Corporation (J+K+L+M+N-O+P) _____

Index